African Plays for Playing I

Plays by Nuwa Sentongo,
Jacob Hevi & 'Segun Ajibade

Selected and edited by
Michael Etherton

D1563344

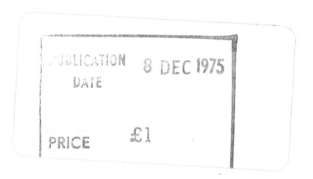

LONDON

HEINEMANN

IBADAN · NAIROBI · LUSAKA

Heinemann Educational Books Ltd
48 Charles Street, London W1X 8AH
P.M.B. 5205 Ibadan · P.O. Box 45314 Nairobi
P.O. Box 3966 Lusaka

EDINBURGH MELBOURNE TORONTO AUCKLAND
SINGAPORE HONG KONG KUALA LUMPUR NEW DELHI

ISBN 0 435 90165 6

Set in 9pt. Baskerville
Printed in Great Britain by
Cox & Wyman Ltd
London, Fakenham and Reading

Contents

Aims of the Anthologies

These anthologies of plays by African writers are for the continent of Africa. Ultimately, the plays themselves are intended for the vast majority of the African people who, in the towns or on the peasant lands, welcome the travelling theatres and the concert parties. Many of those who read these plays have an obligation to produce them.

One aim of these anthologies is to help get more and more people in Africa involved in theatre, both as actors and as audiences. A second less important aim is to make a literary contribution to the growing body of African literature. The qualities that I looked for in the plays to be included in these books were less defined in my own mind and much more complex than they would be for the so-called 'well-made play'. This is not to slight the well-written play, but rather to see it as one of a number of cultural alternatives facing writers and actors in independent African countries.

Who is developing theatre in Africa?

1. Least important are the esoteric remnants of white colonial theatre, and its occasional black middle-class urban offshoots. Very often these groups do not even reflect the metropolitan culture of the French or the British, but rather its meagre provincial expressions.

2. Governments are sponsoring national traditional dance companies, and in the process they are enabling the scope of performance to be broadened on a grand scale.

3. Radio and television employ people for dramatic work on the media, and these people are also often associated with independent theatre companies. Their contribution is generally the modern or contemporary comment; but it is truly national: they broadcast their plays and travel with their companies nationwide. (Some popular concert party professionals are of course wholly maintained as such and do not broadcast, or if they do so it is only very rarely.)

4. The universities, the various colleges and the schools develop drama and theatre activities on a number of levels and through various community agencies.

The point I am anxious to make here concerns the fourth category. In the first place the schools – both primary and secondary – have a much more significant place in the whole process of cultural development than is generally accepted. For a start, one point which needs to be strongly stated is that the moral or intellectual 'suitability' of material for different age groups is completely irrelevant and, worse, often stultifying. It is a concept which runs contrary to the more traditional aspects of the culture anyway. Equally irrelevant is the notion of permitting an inferior standard of performance for and from the school pupil. A third dangerous notion is the concept of a hierarchical structure: the schools at the bottom and the universities at the top. The local school is much closer to the community culturally than the university in the capital many miles away.

If the African University, through the interplay of forces shaping its development, becomes caught up in academic standards defined by universities in the West rather than by criteria evolved by African communities, then it is likely that the most committed and talented students may bravely turn away from it and choose to work with the less inhibited adolescents in – and out of – the schools.

If the schools have an important cultural contribution to make, so do other sections of higher education, notably teacher-training and agricultural and technical colleges. The colleges of technology and the further education colleges train the urban man and orientate him towards a world of development programmes and economic growth. On the other hand, the college of education is often provincially situated and trains teachers for rural primary schools. It has, generally speaking, a rural perspective, and is concerned with the social development of rural communities.

The alternative views of the means by which the growth of African society is achieved are expressed with intensity and passion, and audiences want to hear more from the future practitioners in all these areas.

I speak directly to people in the schools, in teacher training, in agriculture and in technical training, as much as to those already active in theatre in the universities, in professional theatres and on the media. Give these plays to new and wider audiences. They will reflect for them contemporary Africa, in both its local and Pan-African perspectives. Most of these plays have already been performed in the countries where they were written. They deserve wider performance outside these countries, as well as more performances within them.

The plays make direct statements to the audience. All are well conceived showing a close observation of people, an acute awareness of the dramatic situation, and are presented through powerful and poetic dialogue. All are suitable for performance by either professional or amateur companies, with or without theatre experience.

Taken together, the plays demonstrate a wide range of theatrical styles. Some are experiments from which could run many avenues of development. For the moment there are no genres and no dominating styles: everyone is anxious to look at everybody else's work, to share the aims of people in quite different cultural corners, and to build up work which has an appeal for a mass audience drawn from all sections of society.

Unfortunately the true source of professionalism in the African performing arts – dance and music – is not really represented in this anthology, though four of the six plays require songs, dances, and music as an integral part of performance. Eventually African scholars will begin to put together publications containing the musical scores, the choreography, the social references of the various dances, and the dramatic narration of the dance dramas now being developed in many African countries. This work is not wholly traditional. The professional dancers trained in both traditional tribal dances and Western contemporary dance, expand their art into a more inclusive mode of performance. The urban squatters on the fringes of the towns develop sophisticated narrative dances expressing disintegrating relationships to the sounds of instruments improvised from the scrap-heap of the machine civilization. Methods of compiling and presenting such anthologies might have to be radically different from the conventional book, but, hopefully, without too many interpreters between the creative work and its wider performance.

It seems necessary to proceed step-by-step towards some means of communicating the essentially non-verbal aspects of the African theatre genius. A strong response to the plays in this anthology could lead to a much wider exchange of theatre material in Africa.

It is appropriate, though somewhat presumptuous, to put forward suggestions for staging these plays. They are based on my own experience of productions of urban and rural plays in Zambia, and on the experience of others who have been involved over the last ten years in developing travelling theatres in East and West Africa. From the nature of the comments it will be clear that they are not intended to lay down a correct way to present the plays but they might be a starting point. A good text can become a point around which people build their own performance. Through it they can show their talents as individuals and the unique vision of citizens of new nations who wish to share this vision with their fellow citizens.

I am aware that the comments on production which precede most of the plays may well appear obvious or patronizing to those who have inherited theatre facilities left over by the whites and are now doing exciting original theatre work in them. But if you don't start from the essentials – a few actors, a powerful play about things which matter to audiences, some space in a suburban or village compound – how can you be sure you haven't missed something, obliterated a certain African sensibility, lost some indigenous delicate view of things. Dazzling technical innovations can seem all the more desirable to those denied these, particularly if they are denied on some arrogant pretext of not being capable of being competently used. Were the elaborate theatres of America and Europe available in Africa they would be used extremely creatively; but wherever they are provided, it is discovered that they do not necessarily contain the essence of theatre creativity.

The production comments try to focus on what seems to me to be the single most important problem in producing each play. The notes precede each play in order to encourage actors and producers to read the plays with the staging of them in their mind's eye. Some of the plays don't need comments: the text of *Rakinyo* (vol. 1) seems to solve all the problems of production which are raised in the text itself. Other plays for which I have included longer comments are neither less nor more stage-worthy: they raise interesting points of theatrical presentation.

I apologize to the reader who does not like his texts prejudged. The comments are in every instance secondary to the play texts. By contributing them one hopes the plays in the anthology will be produced widely, and that this will encourage others to take up writing and acting and all the other aspects of the performing arts. In this context the metropolitan publisher is in a difficult position because he does not wish to be accused of paternalism towards elements in the popular culture. The aim of this book is to put personalities in African theatre in touch with one another, not to titillate the intellectual middle class in Africa and abroad. There is nothing 'quaint' or 'folksy' about the rapport between popular African playwrights and their audiences.

This is a crucial time for the development of a theatre in Africa. The development of what the industrial societies call the arts is part of the historical process. A unique combination of factors obtain at any given time. The various alternatives perceived and decisions taken reflect the process of social development during that period. A feature of the historical process in Africa at the moment is that it does not have a uniform situation for the whole continent in terms of the movement of political power from the colonial-settler domination to the people of Africa. Because of sophisticated communications these differences are well known. The alternatives for cultural development, which form the basis for the decisions to be taken and the allocation of patronage in the arts, often appear to have contradictions within themselves and are incomprehensible.

An example of this is the mutual determination of both the white South African regime and many independent African governments to develop elements of the traditional ethnic or tribal cultures. For white South Africans, the dances, songs, and plastic arts of the black people in South Africa have become sterile and incapable of any emotional growth. Black governments, on the other hand, see their people's culture as dynamic, and are obliged to recognize opportunities for political organization within the context of cultural expression. The grass-roots members of a political party can communicate with their leaders. Of course, some black governments behave similarly to the South Africans, disassociating the cultural revival from its social milieu – for example the way in which dancers are made to perform for tourists like monkeys in a zoo.

All the writers represented in this anthology have written other plays, and some of these are quite widely performed in the writers' home areas. Many major African playwrights feel a need to move away from the schools, the universities, and the literature curriculum, seeking an audience beyond the walls of the institute in which the new drama activities have been developed. Zambian students travel into the shanty compounds and make contact with local traditional dance groups; Tanzanian students go into factories in Dar es Salaam and make plays with the workers; Ugandan students travel to rural communities. In Nigeria, travelling theatres have won the support and participation of well-known television and radio personalities, and in many instances generated new popular personalities.

Unfortunately, African theatre has come to be judged by the play which is published by the English or French publisher – even though in some instances these plays have never been produced; and if they are subsequently produced it is because of being published, not because they are necessarily good dramatically. It would be even more unfortunate if the literary theatre became the main criterion within Africa, particularly in the minds of those dispensing patronage. For their response would be to distort the appeals of the political leaders, and eventually the potential of African theatre for integration of all levels of society would be lost; the audiences would become again exclusively middle class.

As Kabwe Kasoma says: 'In Africa the theatre must go to the people, rather than expect the people to come to it.'

Please write to the dramatist whose play you perform from this anthology. He or she will be interested to know how you get on and what sort of response you achieve. Heinemann will forward your letters in the first instance, so that you can write to the author

    c/o Heinemann Educational Books,

    48 Charles Street,

    London W1X 8AH.

They control the performance rights and are concerned to be as flexible as possible, bearing in mind the particular concerns of each of the writers whose work is represented in this anthology. Performances may not be given unless permission has been obtained from one of the offices of Heinemann Educational Books.

MICHAEL ETHERTON

The Invisible Bond

NUWA SENTONGO

Some Production Comments

The corpse in this play is a flesh-and-blood actor. How you dress him
up depends on your knowledge as to the way a dead man should look
to the audience before whom you intend performing this play. For
example, there are often ritual clothings for a dead body, and these have
complex symbolism for particular communities. Nuwa Sentongo has
made the corpse of Damulira one which is wrapped in bark-cloth, but it
is much more important that you present the corpse of Damulira in the
way which is most powerful for your audience.

Secret or ritual night-robbing of fresh graves – for whatever reason –
has been known in most societies, though often the taboos are so strong
it is frequently not acknowledged. Producers may have to do some
research in order to discover authentic aspects of the rituals, songs, and
dances of grave-robbers which are nearer to home than the particularly
Ugandan ones given in the text of the play. If you want to keep the human
body-eating theme specifically Ugandan, be careful that your performance
of the play does not become an anti-Ugandan play ('In Uganda they
eat their dead!', 'Ugandans are cannibals!'). This is not Mr Sentongo's
intention at all: his theme, story, and main concern are to show in
concrete terms how a man copes with the physical effects upon himself
of his violation of another man's life. To be faithful to the author's
intentions you should make the play as real as possible for your own
audiences. I am sure that it will have the same success as it had when
performed by Mr Sentongo's own company, the Ngoma Players, at the
National Theatre in Kampala in May 1972.

Technical Suggestions

The Invisible Bond is easy to stage once you have worked out how you are
going to make it clear to your audience that the action of the play is
happening at night. How are your actors going to make night-time
convincing for an audience sitting outside on a hot afternoon? Even at
night your actors must be lit: what lighting indicates daylight and what
lighting indicates night – especially in a rural open-air production?

What you do is largely dictated by what theatre facilities you have and how your audience expects you to use them.

The answer is, of course, to use the particular techniques which your audience are used to. For example, the people who are accustomed to seeing plays in a Western-type theatre building with blackout facilities and a full range of stage lighting, expect you to use them effectively. (Many of them might also be keen for innovation and experiment.) The chances are, however, that the majority of people who might want to present this play to audiences in Africa will not have – or want – access to a Western-type theatre. So how do you create the atmosphere of night, in which a man wrestles with his corpse-victim, in a play which you are taking around villages and performing in school playgrounds or on football pitches or in church halls? What techniques will these people be used to? What will they expect you to do? What conventions can you use which do not need explaining?

It is the style and quality of the acting, and the choice and use of traditional (and even modern) songs, dances, and music, which is all-important. In this respect the actor in Africa is helped by the many symbolic references still vibrant in the local cultural traditions. In both rural and urban areas any sort of performance – the rural traditional dance, the university play, urban pop and soul, radio and television programmes – is at its best a combination of symbols and closely observed realism. A dramatic traditional dance, for example, can combine formal elements which the dancers have rehearsed very carefully, with spontaneous improvisation which the audience in their appreciation encourage the dancers to do. It is a real synthesis because the formal and spontaneous elements cannot be differentiated.

If you transfer this technique of the traditional African dance to the theatrical situation – in this case actors performing a drama of the dead in the blackness of the night – you and your actors will combine the relevant songs, dances, gestures, and behaviour between people in formal roles, with a sensitivity towards your audience's response. The audience will expect to establish some rapport with you the actors, and they will expect you to be sensitive to their responses to what you are doing. After all, they are used to this rapport in the traditional performance situation.

A useful exercise which you, as a group of actors working together on this play, could do is first of all to run through a scene in the play – just a short piece of the story – as though it was happening in the day-time. Then repeat the scene as though it was taking place in the dead of night. Afterwards, discuss together what changes you as individual actors felt had been made in the scene. Were you aware of making any changes at all? This sort of exercise returns you to your own imagination, but it also establishes a creative rapport within the group. The audience will appreciate it very much if you take some time to work out carefully the meaning of your acting. If you convince them that you know what you are doing on the stage they will more actively participate in the performance.

Here are one or two other suggestions which you might find useful:

If you are intending to perform in the open air, in an arena or on a stage which you have had to organize quickly during the afternoon for your performance in the evening, you might consider arranging your acting area and the audience as shown below.

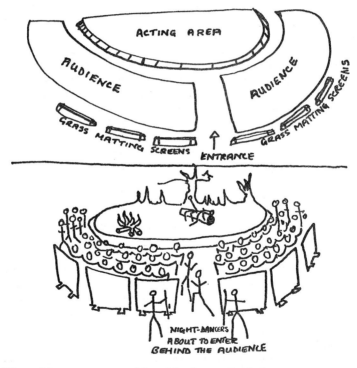

The sudden appearance of the night-dancers behind or alongside members of the audience gives the same sort of shock as finding someone suddenly standing beside you in the dark. Bring the night-dancers in behind the audience absolutely silently just before the preceding scene ends; have them stand perfectly still and silent; and then the moment the other actors have gone off the stage, have them suddenly make their presence felt, perhaps by dangerous sounds or threatening movements. The aim of this particular technique would be to make your audience feel unsettled.

If you are performing outside at night you can also experiment with portable pressure gas lights, with fires, and with flaming torches. For instance, you could build up a couple of big fires one or two hours before your performance is due to begin. As the performance is about to start, the drumming can intensify and members of the cast can suddenly rush on and put out the fires with water. Out of the sudden darkness, steam, hissing smoke, and acrid smells come the mourners bearing the dead body and carrying the gas lamps with their sharp white light. Silhouetted and partly concealed by the swirling smoke are the moving bodies of the night-dancers. It is right that fires should be low or even out for the duration of the performance, because death itself is cold and empty. The audience will be shocked into an awareness of this by the contrast between the friendly firelight and the smokey darkness pierced by the rays of light from the gas pressure lamps.

Incidentally, portable gas pressure lamps (they are known by a number of different brand names) are exciting things to use for many different types of performance, both indoors and in the open air. They can be easily adapted so as to shine only on the players and not into the audience's eyes:

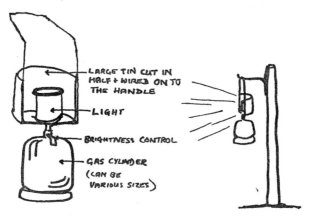

LARGE TIN CUT IN HALF & WIRED ON TO THE HANDLE

LIGHT

BRIGHTNESS CONTROL

GAS CYLINDER (CAN BE VARIOUS SIZES)

You can also put some sand in the bottom of a fairly large paper bag and stand a candle upright in the sand in the bag. Twenty of these, say, can mark off the acting area from the audience and can give some – not much though – soft light near the front of the stage. Ordinary paraffin lamps are also useful and relatively inexpensive. They are not heavy to carry and reasonably safe; and if an actor holds one near to his face he can light his features quite dramatically. These, and of course the gas lamps as well, can be hung on nearby trees or poles in order to illuminate actors from overhead.

Finally, firelight gives good light, is warm, and creates a communal atmosphere. It is best to keep audience and acting areas flexible when performing at night around very big fires, because sometimes the wind changes and of course no member of the audience wants to sit trapped with the smoke blowing up his nostrils. On the other hand, a performance becomes dynamic when actors and audience quite naturally adjust their positions *vis-à-vis* each other in order to get the best warmth and light from the fires.

Having discussed play-lighting for open air performances at night, I feel I should redress the balance by saying that the day-time performance should not be despised at all. Indeed many people feel that the afternoon – when the shops are closed, after the football match, or when the chores on the land have been done – is the right time for performances. If your audience feels this, then you will have no difficulty in making them believe in the night and death themes in the play, providing you use the other cultural references; the songs, the dances, the costumes and the gestures which your audience is most familiar with. Such is the quality of Mr Sentongo's text of *The Invisible Bond* (Vol 1) that with good acting, good songs and dances from your own area, it cannot fail to make an impact on the audience at any time of the day.

The Invisible Bond

CHARACTERS

LEADER OF NIGHT-DANCERS
SECOND NIGHT-DANCER
THIRD NIGHT-DANCER
WOMAN MOURNER
ANOTHER WOMAN MOURNER
FIRST VOICE
SECOND VOICE
THIRD VOICE
FOURTH VOICE
FIFTH VOICE
SIXTH VOICE

SEVENTH VOICE
CORPSE/DAMULIRA
KIBAATE
NIGHT-DANCER'S WIVES:
First Wife
Second Wife
Third Wife
Fourth Wife
FEMALE SINGER
KIBAATE'S WIFE

This text sets the action in Uganda.

This play was first produced by the Ngoma Players at the National Theatre, Kampala, in May 1972. It was directed by Nuwa Sentongo.

SCENE ONE

A graveyard. A group of people come in doing a funeral dirge. A corpse is brought in and laid out for the final ritual. Third night-dancer performs the ritual.

THIRD NIGHT-DANCER: Here's the needle and thread. If anybody calls you, say that you're still sewing your master's clothes.

WOMAN MOURNER: Is that a needle?

THIRD NIGHT-DANCER: What did you say?

WOMAN MOURNER: What did you put there?

THIRD NIGHT-DANCER: Why do you ask?

WOMAN MOURNER: Well I want to know. You should have showed us what you put there. How do we know that it's a needle?

THIRD NIGHT-DANCER: Would you doubt a good neighbour?

WOMAN MOURNER: These days you never know. The world we live in is not a world and the people are no longer people.

THIRD NIGHT-DANCER: The ceremony is over. Everybody go back to your houses.

ANOTHER MOURNER: But we haven't buried our friend.

THIRD NIGHT-DANCER: O.K. Let's bury him. [*They bury him unceremoniously*] That's enough. He's well buried and protected against any mischief.

They go off doing the funeral dirge. One female mourner ecstatically breaks out into frantic tears, and sings a mourning-song in the local language.

FEMALE SINGER: *Mwami twalagana bwababiri nti bwolifa ndikaaba,*
Biribwa nkolentya
Mwami twalagaana bwababiri nti bwolifa ndikaaba,
Biribwa nkole ntya
Omwagalwa, Omuyeyebwa
Biribwa npite ani?
Owekisa Omusutibwa
Biribwa nkole ntya?

Nkolentya Nfudde Omwoyo?
Biribwa nkolentya
Naddawa abange nayita ani?
Biribwa nkolentya?
Omwagalwa, Omuyeyebwa
Owekisa, Omusutibwa
Biribwa nkole ntya?

Yaabade ssebo.
Nayitanga ani nze mmama?

Gweyanjigiriza okwogera
Kati ondesewa nze mmaama?
Mukwano nayita ani?

Baaba twalagana bwababiri
Biribwa nkole ntya
Nti bwolifa ndikaaba
Biribwa nkole ntya
Mukwano twalagana bwababiri nti bwolifa
Ndikaaba
Biribwa mpite ani?
Omwagalwa, Omuyeyebwa
Biribwa nkole ntya

Ondesewa nfudde omwoyo
Biribwa nkole ntya
Nze nayitani abange naddawa
Biribwa nkole ntya

Baaba wandirwaddekono mukwano
Ne ntwalako mu ddwaliro
Ssebo nebajjanjabako
Nemanya olumbe olukusse mukadde

Mukwano twalagaana bwababiri nti
bwolifa ndikaaba   **[repeat]**
Biribwa nkole ntya
Omuwanibwa, Omusutibwa
Biribwa nkole ntya

Baaba mukwano, wasangaki
ngogenze okutabaala?
Singa wamanya ssebo n'otuula
Kwolwo n'otogenda Kutabaala mukamawange.
Kati nze nayita ani,
Nze maama ondese wa?

Baaba twalagaana bwababiri nti
bwolifa ndikaaba   **[repeat]**
Biribwa nkole ntya
Mbasiibula obunaku bunzita
Biribwa nkole ntya
Nze naddawa nfudde omwoyo
Biribwa mpite ani?
Omwanibwa, Omuyeyebwa
Biribwa nkole ntya.

A group of night-dancers run on to the scene, frantically. They start to dance frantically – shouting, singing, laughing, screaming, as though possessed. They dance round the grave many times. One of them, apparently the leader, bends down to the grave and begins to call out.

LEADER OF NIGHT-DANCERS: Damulira, Damulira, Damulira, come out, come out . . . Eh Damulira, come out quick. [*no reply*] I guess he is still very stubborn. Let us dance a few more times, we may arouse him. Not so wild. Wait a moment. Give me that bowl and I'll sprinkle that 'hunter-never-misses'. [*he sprinkles*] It is all right now. You can resume your dances. [*they dance round the grave. After some time, the leader bends down and calls out*] Damulira, Damulira, come out, come out, let us go and hunt monkeys, come out I say. [*feeble voice replies from the grave. The leader is now very excited. He sprinkles more medicine and calls out again*] Damulira, Damulira, come out, quick man, quick, the monkeys are escaping, they have eaten all the maize, come out, let us go and hunt them, here here, right here, oh our maize our lovely maize, quick Damulira, be a good neighbour come out come out . . .

CORPSE [*now loud from the grave*]: O.K. I am coming immediately.

All the night-dancers dance even more ecstatically, anticipating Damulira's arrival. Damulira comes out. He is completely wrapped in bark-cloth. All the night-dancers, except the Leader who is still enjoying the dance by himself, grab Damulira from all sides, shouting their favourite parts of human flesh. Various voices of night-dancers shout:

FIRST VOICE: I'll eat the arm.

SECOND VOICE: The ear is mine.

THIRD VOICE: I like his full-blown lip and the thick chin.

FOURTH VOICE: I'll eat the eyeballs.

FIFTH VOICE: I like these fat buttocks.

SIXTH VOICE: I want the toes.

SEVENTH VOICE: Who will eat the thighs?

LEADER OF NIGHT-DANCERS: Stop! Stop I say! Are you a bunch of hyenas and vultures? Are you human beings or beasts? Don't you have any sense of decency and patience? Now listen to me. We have to do this job in a decent manner. We have three households represented here. Each household must get a fair share according to its size and the part it has played in accomplishing the work. You know that the thighs are the most delicious part on the human body. You know also that tradition has it that the most important person in the group, with a fairly large family, takes the thighs. As your Leader and one who has the largest family, I shall take the thighs.

SECOND NIGHT-DANCER: No you won't. This will be the fourth time you have taken thighs. We can't allow this monopoly. Besides, you haven't done anything except calling Damulira from the grave. Anybody could have done that. But it is I who spotted this man and told you that he is fat and would make a pretty good dish. Then I bewitched him and he died. As for the size of family, you have fifteen people under your roof. I happen to have more uncles and aunts than you. They bring my family up to twenty hungry mouths, so I should take the thighs.

THIRD NIGHT-DANCER: What about me? Both of you are famous night-dancers. Everybody in the village knows you, so they wouldn't allow any of you or your relatives to attend the funeral. But nobody knows that I'm a night-dancer. So, first I convinced the relatives of the deceased that I should perform the funeral rites to protect the corpse against night-dancers. I gave them the wrong medicine which has made it possible for Damulira to come out so quickly.

LEADER OF NIGHT-DANCERS: What are you talking about? You have seen me calling out corpses more than once but have you ever seen me sprinkle this 'hunter–never-misses'?

THIRD NIGHT-DANCER: Of course, you have used it before, when we fetched Gulu.

LEADER OF NIGHT-DANCERS: I know that, but that was because Gulu was such a stubborn corpse. So was Damulira. Your medicine did not make him less stubborn.

THIRD NIGHT-DANCER: But who directed you here? I attended the funeral, and so I got to know the location of the grave and I was able to lead the way. What would you have done without me? As for your talk about the size of the family, it is all rubbish. You, the leader, have the courage to include parents-in-law as members of the household just to suit your convenience. And you, my friend, include nieces, grandchildren, uncles, aunts and neighbours. You don't have twenty people under your roof do you? Why do you always want to cheat me? You know very well that I have children. I am more man than both of you. I should take the thighs.

LEADER OF NIGHT-DANCERS: Take it? I won't allow you. We shall have to fight it out.

A big battle breaks out. They use human bones for weapons. There is cracking of bones, flashes of light, thunder. They exit fighting. Some carry the corpse, but it is not clear which household has carried away the corpse.

SCENE TWO

A corpse lies deserted by the way-side. Kibaate comes up the road and accidentally steps on the corpse. The corpse groans. Kibaate is scared, jumps up and screams loudly.

CORPSE: Please save me, please save, don't leave me here, save me. [*Kibaate tiptoes to the corpse*] Please save me, please save me, don't leave me here, take me . . .

KIBAATE: What are you? Are you a human being?

CORPSE: Save me, take me with you, please . . . please . . .

KIBAATE: What is the matter with you? Has somebody been trying to murder you? Were they Kondos? How many were they? Did they carry guns and pangas and . . .

CORPSE: Don't ask questions. Carry me away please, quickly. Be quick, danger is very near. Do take me to a place of safety. Please, please . . .

KIBAATE: All right I will help you.

Kibaate struggles to carry the corpse. He succeeds and carries it off the scene. Enter night-dancers' wives.

SECOND WIFE: Please Naki stop singing, our husbands must not hear us.

THIRD WIFE: I'm going to sing as long as I have my voice.

SECOND WIFE: Oh no please don't sing. You know we aren't supposed to follow our husbands.

THIRD WIFE: Who says we aren't supposed to follow them?

SECOND WIFE: Don't you know the tradition? When our husbands go to night-dance we are not supposed to follow them except on special occasions, and we have to have special permission. Otherwise we should stay at home to prepare the fire for roasting the corpse.

FOURTH WIFE: Why do you bother with her? She has just got married to a night-dancer and after some time she'll get used to our ways.

FIRST WIFE: [*weaving a mat*]: You are right there.

FOURTH WIFE: I mean there is no need for us to overwork ourselves. I remember when I got married. Yes, on the day of the cooking ceremony. They tied a small parcel in the middle of the roof and caused me to accidentally look up. When I looked up, I felt a change in me and I began to long for human flesh.

THIRD WIFE: Strange the way they do it. In my case, they waited for the cultivation ceremony. Very early in the morning before I began to cultivate, they took me to a strange-looking banana tree and asked me to cut a leaf of that tree. They said that it was part of the cultivation ceremony. As soon as I cut the leaf, I felt strange. During the night I was awakened by a voice calling me. And sure enough my husband's family was there, shaving a corpse. I felt so hungry and the meat was so tasty.

SECOND WIFE: Yes it is always tasty when you have just got married.

FIRST WIFE: What do you think we should do now?

THIRD WIFE: Let us sing a song to welcome our husbands.

SECOND WIFE: You and your husbands.

FIRST WIFE: You can't blame her. She's been married only two weeks.

FOURTH WIFE: Who remembers her first week of marriage?

THIRD WIFE: I do.

FOURTH WIFE: Of course you do. I'm asking my grown-up friends.

SECOND WIFE: For me, I spent the first week trying to remember the many things my aunts taught me in order to please my husband.

FIRST WIFE: Ah those instructions! Do this, and that; don't do this, don't do that. They made me cry.

SECOND WIFE: But I didn't tell you. Well, my husband who was far more experienced than I was, realized that all the time I was trying to memorize the instructions. And I was doing things the wrong way. So he said, 'Don't you worry, within a week you will be experienced'; and he said something like, 'Your aunts must be interesting women. I would like to meet them'.

FOURTH WIFE: Eh, did I tell you the story of the man who took his bride's aunt to bed?

ALL WIVES: No!

FOURTH WIFE: Well, now trap me your ears. At the wedding this man realized that the aunt was more beautiful than the bride. So he decided to pretend not to know anything. As is the custom, the aunt hid under the bed, and waited quietly to prove for herself what happened. But the moment never came. Instead the man deliberately shouted to the bride, 'What am I supposed to do?' The bride was supposed to be a virgin so she couldn't make any suggestions. After about one hour of inactivity, the aunt emerged from under the bed, with the intention of rescuing the situation. So she told the bride to step into another room while she put things right, and I'm sure you know what followed.

THIRD WIFE: What did the aunt say afterwards?

FOURTH WIFE: Well, she called her niece and said, 'A young creeping plant needs a prop'.

THIRD WIFE: Did she go back under the bed?

FOURTH WIFE: Was there any need?

SECOND WIFE: I hear footsteps. Let's run away.

They go off. Kibaate appears on the scene carrying the corpse. It is still wrapped, head and all. He can't carry it any farther. He throws it down, almost falling down himself. The corpse wails.

CORPSE: Oh, oh, oh, oh, oh, uh, uh . . . Oh, oh, you are cruel. Everybody is cruel. [*Kibaate is panting heavily*] Oh, you are very cruel.

KIBAATE: Look here, I am not cruel.

CORPSE: Oh yes you are.

KIBAATE: No I am not.

CORPSE: Yes you are. Why did you throw me down?

KIBAATE: I did not throw you down.

CORPSE: Yes you did. You bu. . . threw me down like an undesirable piece of rubbish.

KIBAATE: You are too heavy for me. I can't carry you any farther. Besides, I don't know where I should take you. I can't go on carrying you for ever.

CORPSE: You told me, didn't you, just now, that you were not cruel.

KIBAATE: So what?

CORPSE: Then help me. Just help me to stand; that'll be enough.

KIBAATE: If I am not cruel, it doesn't follow that I'll be your slave.

CORPSE: Don't misunderstand my words.

KIBAATE: I haven't misunderstood them.

CORPSE: Who told you I want you to be my slave? [*no reply*] Please do help me to stand.

KIBAATE: All right. But let this be the last time because I am tired.

He labours at helping the corpse to stand. The corpse is too heavy for him. His muscles are tensed up; he sighs, pants, sweats, but he manages to make it stand.

CORPSE: How can I thank you? [*Kibaate is still panting too hard to talk*] How can I thank you? You have saved me.

KIBAATE: Saved you?

CORPSE: Yes, you have saved me. Those people wanted to eat me. They came for me and called me out of my grave. I tried to resist. But their power is so great that it pulled me out of the grave. Fancy that, eat me.

KIBAATE: Do you fear being eaten?

CORPSE: Of course. Nobody wants to be eaten.

KIBAATE: But you are a corpse. You are dead.

CORPSE: I am a corpse all right. I am dead I know, you don't have to remind me of that. But I don't want to be eaten, to go down someone's gullet, to be chewed and ground by his molars, then

churned by his stomach and end up in a latrine. That is where you
end up: in a latrine [*Noises are heard off-stage. They start*] What's that?
Are they coming back? Look for me please, will you? [*Kibaate looks
around nervously. There is nothing*] What was it?

KIBAATE: There was nothing, not even the noise.

CORPSE: I thought they had come back. I hate those people. How can
they want to eat me?

KIBAATE: Look here, I must be going. I don't want them to find me
here. They may want to eat me too.

CORPSE: Please don't go. I implore you don't go. Please don't go.

KIBAATE: Well I must save my life.

CORPSE: Then take me with you.

KIBAATE: Take you with me! How can I possibly take you? Where
shall I take you?

CORPSE: Wherever you are going, take me there too. I'll be anything
to you . . . a slave . . . anything you want.

KIBAATE: I have never owned slaves and I don't want to own any
now.

CORPSE: You are my saviour.

KIBAATE: So what?

CORPSE: Then take me with you.

KIBAATE: Look here, I can't take a corpse with me. I am not a night-
dancer like those people.

CORPSE: I am not asking you to eat me. I am asking you to save me
from the night-dancers. Save me!

Kibaate starts to go. The corpse falls down.

CORPSE: Help! Help! Lift me! Help! [*Kibaate comes back and lifts it up. It
holds on to him, but he wants to free himself*] I tell you what, you can
help me, do help me please.

KIBAATE: No, let me go. Don't hold on to me.

CORPSE: Listen! You told me that you love human beings and life, that
you respect human life, that there is nothing more beautiful than
human life, that human life must be saved because it is the only
thing we are left with. You told me all that didn't you. Don't you
remember?

KIBAATE: So what?

CORPSE: Well you can therefore help me.

KIBAATE: I love human beings but not corpses.

CORPSE: But you must help others to live.

KIBAATE: Quite right.

CORPSE: Then help me.

KIBAATE: But you are dead. You are a corpse.

CORPSE: Do you want a corpse to be eaten?

KIBAATE: I have already told you, I don't.

CORPSE: Look at me. Do you want me to be eaten?

KIBAATE: Stop that! It scares me to death!

CORPSE: Then help me.

KIBAATE: Will my help rescue you?

CORPSE: Of course, that is why I asked you. Now come, unwrap my head. [*Kibaate unwraps the head*] Thank you very much. You see my hair?

KIBAATE: It is very filthy.

CORPSE: Of course, what do you expect to happen when a man lies down in the grave without washing his hair? Now I want you to cut it off.

KIBAATE: What?

CORPSE: I want you to cut off this hair and that will save me.

KIBAATE: Save you?

CORPSE: Yes it will save me.

KIBAATE: How do you mean?

CORPSE: Well, when they come back and find me with a clean, shaved head they won't recognize me. They will think it is a completely different corpse.

KIBAATE: What do you take night-dancers for? Idiots? Do you think they have no imagination? Can't they come and grab the nearest corpse, hair or no hair?

CORPSE: I know night-dancers. They fear witchcraft, so they make sure they take the right corpse. But don't let us waste time arguing over simple matters. Come and shave my hair.

KIBAATE: I can't. I haven't got a pair of scissors.

CORPSE: Well, use a razor-blade.

KIBAATE: I haven't got that either.

CORPSE: Use a knife or a panga.

KIBAATE: I haven't got anything.

CORPSE: Oh what shall we do?

Kibaate paces around in contemplation.

KIBAATE: I have got an idea. Suppose I pluck it off with my hands?

CORPSE: Do what?

KIBAATE: Pluck it off with my hands.

CORPSE: Pluck off what?

KIBAATE: Pluck off your hair. You know I haven't got anything to shave it off with, but I can pluck it off with my hands.

CORPSE: Well that is an idea. [*Kibaate gets ready to do the job*] Wait a minute. I want to appear smart, but if you pluck it off with your hands I won't appear all that smart.

KIBAATE: But you are a corpse. What do you want to appear smart for?

CORPSE: I know what you mean. You must in fact be surprised to meet a talking corpse.

KIBAATE: That is not the point.

CORPSE: All the same I'll tell you. Those people have got power over the dead and the living too. When they call you, you can't resist.

KIBAATE: Don't tell me all that, I am scared. I don't want to hear it. Just let me pluck out your hair.

CORPSE: You must listen to my story. I died only four days ago. I had stayed in the grave for only one day when those people came. They never allow the dead any rest or freedom. They come bouncing on us, terrorizing our existence, devil take them. There is no more freedom left to the dead.

KIBAATE: Look here, I don't want to know your story. It is unbearable. Besides, we have got to act quickly otherwise they might give us a big suprise. Let me pluck your hair out.

CORPSE: O.K. [*they both get in position. Kibaate plucks off some hair, only once, but does it very violently. Dust is seen rising from the hair. The corpse jumps up in the air and then falls down violently, wailing. Kibaate is puzzled. After a short while he picks up the corpse and makes it stand*] Oh! oh! You are killing me, you are killing me, you are cruel!

KIBAATE: I am not killing you and I am not cruel.

CORPSE: Yes you are cruel.

KIBBATE: You asked me to do this.

CORPSE: I know I did. But why do it violently? You want to kill me.

KIBAATE: But you are dead, already.

CORPSE: Yes I know I am dead, but don't kill me any further.

KIBAATE: In that case there is nothing I can do for you. I must go home.

Kibaate begins to go. A group of night-dancers appear on the scene. Kibaate is so scared that he runs back to the corpse for security. The night-dancers simply run across as if chasing something. After a little while Kibaate gets scared of the corpse. He lets go of it and the corpse falls down.

CORPSE: Please help me to stand. [*Kibaate helps the corpse to stand*] Ah, that was them. That really was them.

KIBAATE: Yes it was.

CORPSE: Did you see them?

KIBAATE: Yes I did.

CORPSE: Very clearly?

KIBAATE: Yes very clearly.

CORPSE: Now what shall we do?

KIBAATE: Who?

CORPSE: We . . . us . . . you and me.

KIBAATE: As for me I am going back home.

CORPSE: You can't leave me here alone. What shall I do?

KIBAATE: I can't take you with me.

CORPSE: Yes you can.

KIBAATE: No I can't. What will people think?

CORPSE: What does it matter what people think?

KIBAATE: It matters a great deal. They may think that I am a
    night-dancer.

CORPSE: You may be a night-dancer.

KIBAATE: What the devil has put that into your head?

CORPSE: What were you doing in the dead of night?

KIBAATE: I was simply walking.

CORPSE: Walking at this time of the night?

KIBAATE: I am free to do what I want.

CORPSE: Freedom, freedom. You go on believing what you want. Where
    were you going?

KIBAATE: I was going back home.

CORPSE: Where were you coming from?

KIBAATE: What does it matter where? Just leave me alone.

CORPSE: O.K. Let us go.

KIBAATE: Go where?

CORPSE: Wherever you are going.

KIBAATE: I suppose I was destined to carry you, but let this be the last
    time. [*exit*]

Enter wives.

SECOND WIFE: [*calling*]: Uu, uuuu. Uuu, it's all right, you can come out.

The other wives come out.

FIRST WIFE: Oh, oh, my hiding was very bad. How was yours?

THIRD WIFE: I am tired. All I want is my husband.

FOURTH WIFE: You women, we're all being very silly. How can married
    women stay out like this when we are supposed to stay indoors and
    make the fire? Let's go back home.

THIRD WIFE: How can we go back home without our husbands?

FOURTH WIFE: You will soon get used to that.

SECOND WIFE: Yes, tell her that she'll soon have to spend nights alone in the house. And when her husband comes back the following day and she asks him where he spent the night, he will beat her.

FIRST WIFE: Don't frighten the young woman. Her husband is a very domesticated man.

SECOND WIFE: Don't they all start by being domesticated?

FIRST WIFE: Maybe they do. But on the whole night-dancers make good husbands. They spend the nights hunting meat for us, unlike the other men. Secondly, most women fear to be friends with night-dancers so they mostly stay at home with their wives.

FOURTH WIFE: I don't agree with you there because my husband hardly stays at home. He mixes very well with the villagers.

SECOND WIFE: Eh Mala, when will you finish that mat? You've been working on it for over a year now.

FIRST WIFE: Please Akon, stop your exaggeration. You know I'm always working on a mat and this is a new one. I started it only two weeks ago.

SECOND WIFE: That's not true. It can't be true.

FIRST WIFE: But it's true.

SECOND WIFE: No . . . no . . . you've been weaving that mat for about one year now.

FOURTH WIFE: You know Akon, that isn't true.

THIRD WIFE: Eh women, I hear our husbands' voices.

FOURTH WIFE: Then let's hide – quick.

THIRD WIFE: Why should we hide? Those men are our husbands. We must wait here and welcome them.

FIRST WIFE: You know we have to hide because we're supposed to be at home . . .

FOURTH WIFE: Why do you waste our time explaining? Let's drag her to a hiding place before they find us.

SECOND WIFE: Yes, that's right.

THIRD WIFE: No, don't drag me, stop it, stop it . . .

FOURTH WIFE: Be a good woman and stop shouting.

They drag her off. Night-dancers appear on the scene.

LEADER OF NIGHT-DANCERS: I smell my wife.

NIGHT-DANCER: I can smell mine too.

LEADER OF NIGHT-DANCERS: Eh, what are they up to?

NIGHT-DANCER: I can't tell.

LEADER OF NIGHT-DANCERS: Women, come out wherever you are. Come out before I beat you. Come out.

NIGHT-DANCER: Are you mad?

LEADER OF NIGHT-DANCERS: Why mad?

NIGHT-DANCER: How do you know they are here?

LEADER OF NIGHT-DANCERS: Can't you smell them?

NIGHT-DANCER: I think he is on heat!

LEADER OF NIGHT-DANCERS: Come out women, come out . . .

NIGHT-DANCER: Why don't you leave the women alone?

LEADER OF NIGHT-DANCERS: Aren't they women? How do you expect men to leave women alone?

NIGHT-DANCER: But we have something important to do.

NIGHT-DANCER: Yes, we have to find the corpse.

LEADER OF NIGHT-DANCERS: Women, come out, come out I say. I can see you wherever you're hiding.

NIGHT-DANCER: Where do you think we can find that corpse? We have searched all the possible places but in vain.

NIGHT-DANCER: I didn't know Damulira was such a stubborn corpse.

NIGHT-DANCER: What shall we tell our wives?

NIGHT-DANCER: Yes, that is the problem now. They must have prepared the fire now expecting that we shall take them some meat.

NIGHT-DANCER: Your wife isn't as bad as mine. Mine ho . . . ho . . . if I don't take any meat she'll refuse to give me food.

NIGHT-DANCER: Yours' is at least weak. But mine, you remember how she beat me last week?

LEADER OF NIGHT-DANCERS: Well, I can't find the bloody women.

NIGHT-DANCER: I told you the women weren't here.

NIGHT-DANCER: We can at least get peace.

LEADER OF NIGHT-DANCERS: If I had found them I would've beaten the whole lot of them.

NIGHT-DANCER: You had better help me to beat mine.

LEADER OF NIGHT-DANCERS: Yes, I remember yours is a very tough woman. But I will never allow any woman to beat me. You see me! Never will a woman ever beat me . . .

The wives of the night-dancers appear.

SECOND WIFE: So that's what you've been doing all the time, backbiting us, and the corpse escaped. What sort of men are you?

FOURTH WIFE: Yes, what sort of men are you?

The wives address their respective husbands. The couples are on different parts of the stage.

SECOND WIFE: When we heard your voices, we began to beat our stomachs, that at last meat has come. Now where's the meat?

LEADER OF NIGHT-DANCERS: Woman, mind your own business.

SECOND WIFE: Isn't it my business to demand meat for cooking?

LEADER OF NIGHT-DANCERS: Shut up.

FOURTH WIFE: Honestly, you men, what use are you to us? What shall we eat today? I think we should take over the hunting.

NIGHT-DANCER: Listen woman, in our cult, women don't go hunting human flesh. Of course they're free to night-dance on the . . .

NIGHT-DANCER: Oh my darling, dearest sweet palm thorn, are you still all right?

THIRD WIFE: Yes, darling, I have been waiting all this time.

NIGHT-DANCER: You know I almost missed my friends, I mean they almost left me behind. I was thinking about you, then I forgot what I was doing and I forgot where I was.

THIRD WIFE: You forgot all these because of me?

NIGHT-DANCER: Yes, because of you.

THIRD WIFE: Oh that's wonderful darling. You know these women almost beat me up for talking about you all the time.

NIGHT-DANCER: Really! So you've been talking about me.

FOURTH WIFE: I'm not going to talk to you unless you give me something to eat.

NIGHT-DANCER: It's you who should give me something to eat.

FOURTH WIFE: Who? Me? You left us, poor women, at home, and told us that you were going to bring us meat. And here we are, still waiting for your meat so that we can feast. When you have failed to get the meat you say women must feed you.

NIGHT-DANCER: This is the best mat you've ever made.

FIRST WIFE: Thank you dear. I've been working on it for such a long time now. But wait until I finish it.

NIGHT-DANCER: What will happen?

FIRST WIFE: It's going to be yours', in memory of our wedding.

NIGHT-DANCER: That's why I will always love you. I chose the right kind of woman. But tell me, how do you manage to weave this mat at night. Can you see what you're weaving?

FIRST WIFE: Of course, the moon is bright. Anyway, you should forget that and only remember that the mat is in remembrance of our wedding.

NIGHT-DANCER: I can never understand you. How can you remember the wedding after such a long time?

FIRST WIFE: How can I forget such an important event?

NIGHT-DANCER: Do you remember how I first met you?

THIRD WIFE: Of course I do.

NIGHT-DANCER: Of course I don't expect you to forget. I had been asked by these men to come and bewitch you so that we could eat you.

THIRD WIFE: Is that so?

NIGHT-DANCER: Yes, it is true. But as I approached, I heard you singing that lovely song. Do you remember it? Well, can you sing it for me now?

Third Wife sings.

LEADER OF NIGHT-DANCERS: You men, it's almost morning, I mean dawn. Let us go and look for Damulira.

NIGHT-DANCER: Yes but give us one more minute.

LEADER OF NIGHT-DANCERS: No . . . no . . . no . . . let's go.

WIVES: We should also come.

LEADER OF NIGHT-DANCERS: No you can't.

NIGHT-DANCER: This time let us try to plan what we are going to do.

LEADER OF NIGHT-DANCERS: What do you mean, plan?

NIGHT-DANCER: Well, there are questions we must ask before we set off. For instance, where should we go? Where is the corpse likely to be hiding? What caused our failure, in the first instance?

NIGHT-DANCER: You know we forgot something. After getting the corpse, we should have walked backwards like this . . .

FOURTH WIFE: Oh stop, stop! You mustn't do that.

NIGHT-DANCER: Why not?

FOURTH WIFE: Have you already forgotten? This is the first time he has gone out hunting since his wedding. And you know he mustn't walk backwards before the ghee-returning ceremony has been performed.

NIGHT-DANCER: By the way, when are you planning to return the ghee?

NIGHT-DANCER: I don't know when because I'm required to take thighs as well.

LEADER: Look here, if we ever catch Damulira, I'm going to eat the thighs.

NIGHT-DANCER: Let's not quarrel about Damulira's thighs again. The most important thing is to get hold of the corpse.

NIGHT-DANCER: But you've got to consider my problem.

LEADER OF NIGHT-DANCERS: What's your problem?

NIGHT-DANCER: Do you know Kibaate?

LEADER OF NIGHT-DANCERS: You mean the shopkeeper who has that young delicious wife?

NIGHT-DANCER: Yes that one. She has the right kind of thighs which my parents-in-law will accept.

LEADER OF NIGHT-DANCERS. What do you want us to do?

NIGHT-DANCER: Let us fetch her now.

NIGHT-DANCER: But she isn't dead.

NIGHT-DANCER: Have you forgotten that I have the mosquito food? All I need is to sit on a coil and call out her spirit. Once the spirit comes, we put it in the coil and then call out the corpse.

LEADER AND OTHER NIGHT-DANCERS: Hey – let's go, let's go . . .

They dance ecstatically, their wives dancing with them, and they exit off the stage dancing. Kibaate appears carrying the corpse.

CORPSE: Oh, oh, you're still very cruel. Yes you're very cruel. [*no reply*] Hey, mister, get me something to sit on.

KIBAATE: What?

CORPSE: Get me something to sit on.

KIBAATE [*he exclaims as he leaves*]: My God! I have never seen such a restless corpse!

CORPSE [*drawing the bark-cloth to itself*]: Oh it is very cold out here. This part of the world is just hell. How do the people of this place manage to live? Cold all the time. I need more bark-cloth to keep warm.

Kibaate comes back with a bench.

KIBAATE: Now don't say again that I'm cruel. I did what I could. I ran all over the place and found this bench. Sit down and let me go. [*Kibaate tries to settle the bench, but the bench will not settle*].

CORPSE: Are you so nervous that you can't even settle the bench?

KIBAATE: I'm not nervous.

CORPSE: Then why can't you settle it?

KIBAATE: Give me time. [*after some time Kibaate manages to settle the bench*] There you are. It is all yours.

CORPSE: O.K. sit me down.

Kibaate sits the corpse down on the bench.

KIBAATE: Are you all right now?

CORPSE: How can I be all right?

KIBAATE: Well, all you wanted was to sit down, and I've brought you the bench. You aren't even grateful.

CORPSE: This isn't a good place. I am very cold.

KIBAATE: I'm also cold.

CORPSE: But you aren't dead are you?

KIBAATE: Not yet.

CORPSE: Then why are you cold?

KIBAATE: Nights in this place are usually very cold. I used to chase girls on such nights, hiding under banana trees, and beating off mosquitos. But now I'm married I can't do such things.

CORPSE: I also used to enjoy such nights, although in my case there were no girls to chase. All girls hated me. But I used to stand out in my courtyard and feel the fresh air. But these days living people must be scared of night-dancers.

KIBAATE: That's true, and Kondos as well. You can't just stand out like that.

CORPSE: What's all this talk about Kondos? There weren't Kondos at the time when I died.

KIBAATE: Then you must have died a long time ago.

CORPSE: But I died only four days ago, on the day people went to the general elections.

KIBAATE: Which elections are you talking about?

CORPSE: I mean the elections of our leaders.

KIBAATE: Then you died ten years ago.

CORPSE: Is it all that bad?

KIBAATE: What do you mean bad?

CORPSE: I mean about the elections . . . no, no, I mean to have been dead for ten years and my memory and all that.

KIBAATE: Well, I must be going home.

CORPSE: So you are deserting me?

KIBAATE: It isn't deserting you. I must go home. This isn't my home.

CORPSE: It isn't mine either.

KIBAATE: So let me go.

CORPSE: Since it belongs to neither of us, we might as well go together or stay together.

KIBAATE: That isn't logical.

CORPSE: I know, but even our presence here is illogical.

KIBAATE: How do you mean?

CORPSE: You remember how we met? It was just by accident. It was by accident that those night-dancers called me out of my grave. It was by accident that a fight broke out and they dropped me on the way. It was by accident that you came along.

KIBAATE: I can see that.

CORPSE: Then relax, sit down, perhaps another accident will happen.

KIBAATE: And they will come back?

CORPSE: Don't say that. Say that the Messiah will come.

KIBAATE: The Messiah?

CORPSE: Yes all we need is the Messiah to deliver us from these mad night-dancers. Oh Messiah, the Almighty, come and deliver us from these monsters! Come and bring peace and love among your people. We are waiting for you, your obedient servants.

KIBAATE: Amen, thank you for the prayer.

CORPSE: Did you like it?

KIBAATE: Yes very much. I wished you would go on and on.

CORPSE: Thank you. Come and share the bench with me.

KIBAATE: No I can't.

CORPSE: O.K. I will sit. You may do whatever you want for the present, but you must be within hearing distance so that I can call you whenever I want.

Kibaate tries to find his way back home. He only manages to go round in circles, and he ends up at the side of the corpse, by accident.

CORPSE: I knew you would come back even without my calling you.

KIBAATE: So it is you again?

CORPSE: Yes it is me.

KIBAATE: Are you everywhere?

CORPSE: No. I'm only here.

KIBAATE: How do you move?

CORPSE: What do you mean?

KIBAATE: I mean how did you come here?

CORPSE: You brought me here.

KIBAATE: No I didn't.

CORPSE: Yes you did. And you left me sitting here. I have been sitting here all the time. You remember leaving me here don't you?

KIBAATE: I remember leaving you at that horrible place where I dropped you, but not here. I am trying to go back home but I have lost my way.

CORPSE: You may go on losing your way; that is your business. As for me, I have been sitting here all the time. You had deserted me but now you have come back.

KIBAATE: By the way, are you the same corpse?

CORPSE: What are you saying?

KIBAATE: I am asking whether you are the same corpse I was carrying.

CORPSE: How can I answer such a silly question? And, stop calling me a corpse. [*pause*] I'm Damulira.

KIBAATE: Oh really! Are you the Damulira I used to know?

CORPSE: Don't be silly.

KIBAATE: I'm not silly.

CORPSE: Shut up!

KIBAATE: Look here, do you remember the way to my home?

CORPSE: This is your home.

KIBAATE: It isn't my home. How can it be my home? How can this be anybody's home? [*Kibaate tries to find the way in silence*]

CORPSE: Hey mister, what's your name?

KIBAATE: I have no name.

CORPSE: You must have a name.

KIBAATE: I have got no name.

CORPSE: Shall I give you one?

KIBAATE [*still searching*]: I don't want it.

CORPSE: Aren't you my friend? Aren't we friends?

KIBAATE: I suppose we are. But what the hell has a name got to do with it?

CORPSE: If we are friends I must call you by a proper name. I remember it now, yes you told me, you are Kibaate.

KIBAATE: I am not.

CORPSE: Yes you're.

KIBAATE: Go hang!

CORPSE: Kibaate!

KIBAATE: Yes?

CORPSE [*is animated, jumps, and happily runs to Kibaate*]: You have accepted it, you have accepted the name. We are friends now. [*The corpse embraces him. He is scared. They both fall down. Kibaate tries to disentangle himself*] Do you want to desert me brother?

KIBAATE: Look here, I have to go home. My wife is waiting.

CORPSE: So you are married?

KIBAATE: Of course, I have told you already.

CORPSE: You are lucky aren't you? When I was in the world, no woman ever loved me. They wouldn't even look at me. They always scorned and abused me with all sorts of names – ape, chimpanzee, gorilla, hippo, pig, frog and many others. How I longed to love a woman, to feel that I loved her and she loved me, to hold her in my arms and rest her body on my chest and feel her breath. I wanted to fondle and feel a woman's full blown breasts, to suckle the nipples and be nourished with the emotion. I wanted to cuddle a woman, to be sweet to her and she to me. One girl loved me. I courted her and almost married her, but she died of a plague. Perhaps you remember that severe plague which swept many villages. There were just too many mice. Then another girl loved me and I nearly married her, but she died of a disease which she got from her grandpa.

KIBAATE: You know, you make feel that this world is unkind. But I must leave you now. [*he begins to go*]

CORPSE: So you are deserting me brother?

KIBAATE: I have already told you. I have to go home because my wife is waiting for me. She has just brewed some banana juice for me.

CORPSE: How do you know?

KIBAATE: I just know it.

CORPSE: Oh you are really lucky. How I longed for the banana juice.

KIBAATE: You longed for it?

CORPSE: I will tell you. [*painfully stands up and moves about ruminatively*] I had spent all the day in the forest looking for the ancestral pole to be fixed in the centre of my hut. I left home without drinking water because the waterpot was empty. I got lost in the forest. I wandered the length and breadth of the forest till the cool evening breeze carried human voices to my ears. They were brewing banana juice. I began to run towards the human figures to beg for some banana juice, but the nearer I ran towards them the further away they went. I chased and chased them in the thick emptiness of the forest, dodging huge trees and creeping plants. I ran and ran and ran.

KIBAATE: Settle down on this bench and don't move. Don't excite yourself.

CORPSE: Can you do me a favour?

KIBAATE: What is it this time?

CORPSE: Can you bring me some banana [*pause*] leaves?

KIBAATE: Banana leaves.

CORPSE: Yes banana leaves.

KIBAATE: What for?

CORPSE: Don't ask questions and please do bring them quickly. [*Kibaate goes to fetch the banana leaves*] How long shall I stay in this horrible place? It started as a dream, someone calling my name. I answered. He ordered me to walk. I walked and here I am. I blame it on my relatives who didn't perform the necessary funeral rites. They should have put a needle and a piece of thread there. [*Kibaate brings some banana leaves*] That's very good, thank you. That is very kind of you, please scatter them all over here. Do as I say and don't ask questions, and do it quickly. [*Kibaate scatters the leaves*] Thank you very much. That will save me.

KIBAATE: Well I must be going home.

CORPSE: Going home? Why should you leave at this crucial moment? Listen. [*noise of people shouting, singing, running*] Cover yourself with banana leaves.

KIBAATE: What are you saying?

CORPSE: Not so loud.

KIBAATE: What did you say?

CORPSE: Cover yourself with banana leaves.

KIBAATE: What for?

CORPSE: Don't ask questions. Just do what I say and do it quickly.

KIBAATE: But I can't fit in any of the banana leaves.

CORPSE: Take quite a number of them.

KIBAATE: How shall I hold them?

CORPSE: How do you mean?

KIBAATE: Well I have only two hands, yet you want me to hold many.

CORPSE: Just throw them on your head and your back.

KIBAATE: Suppose they miss?

CORPSE: Damn your questions.

They both cover themselves with banana leaves. The night-dancers appear on the scene still possessed. The leader calls out:

LEADER OF NIGHT-DANCERS: Damulira, Damulira, come out. Where are you hiding? I can see you wherever you are hiding. Did I animate you to run away from me? And do you think you can manage to escape? Have you forgotten our journey? Look at all these banana leaves. Our enemies must have been here before us. Let us go. [*they dance off*]

CORPSE: Hooray, hooray, it has worked! It has worked!

KIBAARE: What has wotked?

CORPSE: It has worked, it has worked, it has . . .

KIBAATE: What has worked?

CORPSE: It has worked. Don't you see, don't you understand you fool?

KIBAATE: What has worked?

CORPSE: The trick.

KIBAATE: The trick?

CORPSE: Yes the banana leaves. They thought the corpse has already been eaten and that this was a wrong place.

KIBAATE: Well I must be going back to my children.

CORPSE: So you are a father?

KIBAATE: Yes.

CORPSE: How many?

KIBAATE: Two, a boy and a girl, and my wife is now pregnant.

CORPSE: Oh my, you are really lucky. God's been very kind to you.

KIBAATE: But that is the easiest thing in the world. All married people, even unmarried ones, get children. I don't see any luck about it.

CORPSE: Oh those swollen wombs in the Kapeka dispensary! Those tender rosy skins, screaming as the nurses wash them. Those malaria-stricken, sore-throated angels coming in for quinine injections. Those *kwashiorkor* bellies coming in for powder-milk rations. Oh how I waited for those warm bridges of generations. But they didn't come. Not for me.

KIBAATE: All you needed was a woman.

CORPSE: I have told you all women rejected me, because I was suffering from thyroid. I got it at the age of fifteen years. At that time I weighed 150 lbs. but within one month only I began to weigh 400 lbs.

KIBAATE: 400 lbs.?

CORPSE: Yes 400 lbs. I spent one year in bed in Mulago Hospital but I didn't regain my former size and shape, I became some sort of a hippo.

KIBAATE: Then how did you manage to live?

CORPSE: Well, I survived on tranquillizers but I never really recovered. When I died I was so heavy that a crowd of about fifty people carried me to the grave.

KIBAATE: Impossible. You are making up stories.

CORPSE: They thought that I was too heavy to be called out of the grave by any night-dancers, so they didn't perform the necessary funeral rites. But when I was in the grave something strange happened. I became very thin and light as you can see.

KIBAATE: You are too damn heavy.

CORPSE: But you can carry me alone by yourself.

KIBAATE: I am sorry I can't stay any longer to listen to your incredible stories. [*Kibaate begins to go*]

CORPSE: Please can you do me a favour?

KIBAATE: No I am going home.

CORPSE: Just one favour please.

KIBAATE: What is the favour?

CORPSE: Will you cut off my finger-nails?

KIBAATE: No I can't. I have told you I haven't got a razor-blade or a knife.

CORPSE: Can't you bite them with your teeth?

KIBAATE: What about you? [*he forces the corpse's mouth open*] What are these teeth doing? Why don't you bite your own finger-nails?

CORPSE: You see the teeth are there all right but they are rotten. During the time I spent down in the grave all my teeth rotted. It isn't easy to keep your teeth intact in that place.

KIBAATE: I am sorry I can't help you.

CORPSE: Will you take me back to the bench?

KIBAATE: No I won't. I'm not your slave.

CORPSE: O.K. We shall see. [*The corpse becomes animated. It attacks Kibaate, piercing him with its finger-nails. They both fall on to the ground. Kibaate can't disentangle himself. He cries loudly. The corpse stands up over him gaining a commanding position.*] You have to do what I tell you.

KIBAATE: That isn't fair. I was walking back home when I met you. You asked me to save you to carry you away from danger. I did. And now you want to enslave me. Is this your gratitude?

CORPSE: It is because you are stubborn. What are you fidgeting for? Keep still. Don't move until I tell you to. [*he stands*] Now clean my finger-nails quickly before I strike you. [*Kibaate cleans one finger-nail using the corpse's garment*] Don't play tricks on me.

KIBAATE: Leave me alone. Kill me if you want.

CORPSE: I tell you what, gather up all these banana leaves and return them where you got them from.

KIBAATE: I don't remember the place.

CORPSE: You must.

KIBAATE: Devil, why don't you leave me alone? What do you want with me?

CORPSE: I can't leave you alone. You are my subject.

KIBAATE: I am not your subject.

CORPSE: What?

KIBAATE: I am not your subject.

CORPSE: How dare you say that? I order you to say yes.

KIBAATE: No.

CORPSE: Say yes.

KIBAATE: No.

CORPSE: Say yes.

KIBAATE: Yes I am your subject.

CORPSE: Oh come my dear. I am glad I have got a subject. [*the corpse embraces Kibaate. Kibaate is disgusted*] I am really happy. I have searched for a subject for a very long time. I am glad you have accepted the responsibility. You know I was a subject to my father, and the kind of education he subjected me to – always to agree with him or he beats me if I don't. When he died I longed for a subject. I wanted somebody upon whom I could demonstrate my power, some sort of personal reassurance. From now on, as my subject, you will speak with and in my voice, and you mustn't say anything without my permission. You must be proud, because I am very proud of you. Cheer up my dear boy. What is the matter? Don't you want to be my subject?

KIBAATE: What does it matter what I want? You have enslaved me.

CORPSE: I guess it doesn't really matter, so long as you do what I say. Let us go.

KIBAATE: Where shall we go?

CORPSE: Don't ask questions. You just carry me and be quick.

Kibaate obeys the corpse, and carries him off the stage. Fourth wife appears.

FOURTH WIFE: Uuuu. [*calling others*] Come, come come, come I have news. [*the wives come onto the stage.*]

ALL WIVES: What is it?

FOURTH WIFE: When we left you here, I followed our husbands.

THIRD WIFE: I see, how is my sweet husband?

SECOND WIFE: Why don't you let her finish the story?

THIRD WIFE: I thought she was going to tell us about our husbands. That's all I want to hear.

FOURTH WIFE: Let me finish my story. As I was saying, I followed our husbands. They went directly to Kibaate's house and called out Kibaate's wife.

FIRST WIFE: You mean that delicious woman?

FOURTH WIFE: Of course.

THIRD WIFE: Now what will he do without his wife?

SECOND WIFE: What are you commenting for? Don't you know that we are going to feast tonight – u . . . hu . . . huu . . . hu!

ALL WIVES [*very jubilant*]: Uh . . . uhu . . . [*rejoicing and dancing*]

FOURTH WIFE: Stop, stop . . . let's go home and make the fire . . . there must be feasting tonight.

They dance off noisily – Kibaate reappears carrying the corpse.

CORPSE: Ah, that is much better. [*Kibaate is still panting for breath*] Will you do me a favour? [*Kibaate is still panting for breath*]

KIBAATE: I'm tired of doing you favours.

CORPSE: Bring me some food. I want to eat.

KIBAATE: Look here, you are a corpse.

CORPSE: I know, but somehow, I feel different. I feel I'm partly living. Anyway, do get me something to eat.

KIBAATE: How much?

CORPSE: Ha, that reminds me. Put me on to the bench then I'll tell you a story. [*Kibaate puts the corpse on to the bench*] Sit down with me. [*Kibaate sits down*] The bench is rather soft now.

KIBAATE: What?

CORPSE: With you sitting here the bench has become soft and very comfortable to sit on.

KIBAATE: What story did you want to tell me?

CORPSE: I mean I am now comfortable. We should be sitting here like this, always. It is very pleasant.

KIBAATE: Tell me the story.

CORPSE: Oh yes, I was forgetting. I had a neighbour who was a hawker, selling clothes and other humble articles. He used to go along the streets shouting, 'Best wear, you buy from me you get your money's worth, best Jinja Textile, good bitenge at cheap price, buy now, buy cheap . . .' and so on and so forth. After a day's shouting he would go home with a full stomach. This man was a great gourmand. He would eat a bunch of matoke by himself.

KIBAATE: You are pulling my leg.

CORPSE: What?

KIBAATE: I said you are pulling my leg.

CORPSE: Well if you want I will do it. [*the corpse grabs him by the leg and pulls him along*]

KIBAATE: Stop, stop, what is the matter with you?

CORPSE: Which matter?

KIBAATE: You don't know the simplest idioms. I didn't mean I wanted my leg pulled.

CORPSE: In that case I will pull your arm. Here we go. [*the corpse grabs his arm and pulls him along*]

KIBAATE [*shouting from the ground*]: Leave me alone, leave me alone, I hate you I hate . . .

CORPSE [*kicks him*]: Stop that. You have no right to hate me. I am your master and you must do what I say. . Get me some food.

KIBAATE: Where shall I get it from?

CORPSE: Isn't your home near by?

KIBAATE: How do I know? How can I tell? I have lost my sense of direction. I don't know how to get away from this place.

CORPSE: Don't worry. We shall both stay here. I like you very much. You have given me some sort of life. You have given me some sort of awareness. It is more than the feeling of pain or happiness. It is the desire to know, feel, breathe, touch, taste . . . do you understand?

KIBAATE: How can I understand?

CORPSE: The four days I was dead I lost my senses. When the night-dancers invaded me I regained my sense of fear and pain. But with you here it is something different. I feel I have regained my power to think, to be curious, to want to taste and be involved. I can remember the past. It unfolds itself to me.

KIBAATE: How do you mean?

CORPSE: Well it started in Magwala village. I convinced the villagers

that Magwala needed a social club. But the social club to prosper
needed a respectable building. People trusted me because they knew
I was suffering from thyroid and therefore not as worldly as others.
So they gave me the money very easily. After collecting a hundred
thousand shillings, I escaped to Kapeka where I built my own
cotton ginnery.

KIBAATE: Oh my, you built a cotton ginnery? How big is it?

CORPSE: It was fairly big but didn't last long for I didn't know how to
manage it. An Indian bought me out of business.

KIBAATE: Then how did you subsist after that?

CORPSE: I worked in the Kapeka dispensary as a clerk registering
patients who visited the dispensary. Not well-paid but it supported
me for the rest of my life.

KIBAATE: Well I must be going home.

CORPSE: Didn't you like my story?

KIBAATE: That isn't the point.

CORPSE: Please don't go, don't go. How I hate loneliness, not because
I fear the night-dancers, but because I want to talk, to express
myself, to communicate, to get across to people, to pass my message
on to somebody, to whoever cares to listen and it seems you are
listening. But I don't know what this something is, and I don't even
know whether it exists. Do you understand what I am saying?

KIBAATE: I can't make head or tail of what you are saying.

CORPSE: The more I talk to you the more I like to talk and the more I
feel that there is some power which doesn't like me to talk. Therefore
I feel that something is about to happen. Something is bound to
happen. We are only waiting for the moment. I feel a sense of
anxiety and restlessness in me. At this moment something is forcing
me to be nervous. Do you know what it is?

KIBAATE: How can I know?

CORPSE: I feel the earth is moving. Don't you feel it? Don't you feel the
earth moving? Don't you feel the earthquake? Don't you . . . feel . . .
the . . .

*The corpse collapses and falls down. Kibaate is dismayed. He tries to feel the
earth but the earth is firm. There is nothing strange. He goes to the corpse and
helps it to stand.*

KIBAATE: Are you all right?

CORPSE: Yes I am.

KIBAATE: I warned you not to excite yourself.

CORPSE: I haven't excited myself. Did you shave my hair?

KIBAATE: No I had no scissors.

CORPSE: Did you cut my finger-nails?

KIBAATE: No I had no razor-blade.

CORPSE: Did you bring me food?

KIBAATE: No I didn't know where to find it.

CORPSE [*he belches and Kibaate avoids the bad breath*]: But my stomach is full.

KIBAATE: It is full of maggots.

CORPSE: Are you holding me; I mean are you supporting me?

KIBAATE. No. I am standing away from you.

CORPSE: So I can stand on my own. Let me try to walk. [*wobbles around*] Yes, I have managed to walk.

KIBAATE: But you have walked many times since we have been here.

CORPSE: Maybe I have, but I haven't been conscious of it. I didn't think about it. Now I am trying to think about whatever I do.

KIBAATE: It is strange that when you decide to use your mind you wobble like a child just beginning to try his feet. It seems you are growing backwards, beginning your life cycle once again.

CORPSE: Yes I have to begin somewhere. I'll try again.

Corpse wobbles. Kibaate sings.

KIBAATE: *Omwana alitambuladdi? jjo jjuzi*
Omwana alitambuladdi? jjo jjuzi

The corpse falls down. It is furious.

CORPSE: I knew you would come back.

KIBAATE: You again, are you everywhere? Oh I am exhausted. I wish I could smoke my pipe.

CORPSE: So you smoke a pipe?

KIBAATE: Yes I do, mainly to keep awake. You see it was my father. He was always sleepy and I got his sleepiness.

CORPSE: Do you feel sleepy now?

KIBAATE: How can I? You don't give me any rest.

CORPSE: That is because you are stubborn. You must surrender to me and carry out my wishes.

KIBAATE: No I won't surrender.

CORPSE: O.K. Smoke your pipe. Who has stopped you?

KIBAATE: You, you are holding me here and you have sapped my senses.

CORPSE: By the way did you hear the story of the old granny?

KIBAATE: No.

CORPSE: I will tell you. [*corpse wobbles around as it narrates*] There she was on the Nile, puffing, the old granny, she puffed, and watched the spirals of smoke disappear into the full ethereal emptiness. She counted pebbles as she puffed. Arranged them in numerous circles. The honey of the fish flowed. It flowed indifferently granny or no granny. Then she spat, unblocked the pipe, pondering, puzzled. Where does the honey come from? Where does it go? The white egrets drank and bathed innocently as the honey of the fish flowed. It flowed indifferently, egrets or no egrets, she threw a pebble into the Nile to provoke and disturb its calmness, and dipped her foot into the Nile. Ripples formed, then disappeared as the honey of the fish flowed. It flowed indifferently, granny or no . . . [*the corpse collapses. Kibaate drags it back on to the bench*]

KIBAATE: Are you all right?

CORPSE: Yes.

KIBAATE: I told you to sit down and not excite yourself. Let me adjust your bark-cloth.

CORPSE: Thank you very much. That is why I need you, to look after me.

KIBAATE: Well it won't be for long. I have got to go home.

CORPSE: Forget it. You are my subject. Take this bench on the other side, I am tired of sitting on this side.

KIBAATE: No. I won't have anything to do with either the bench or you.

CORPSE [*bursts out*]: Will you take this bench there? [*Kibaate is so frightened that he obeys promptly but he ignores the corpse*] Will you take me to the bench? [*Kibaate obeys*] Well, there seems to be more light in this place.

KIBAATE: Don't be romantic.

CORPSE: I am not romantic. Don't you see that light?

KIBAATE: I can see it now. [*Kibaate looks up at the sky, searching for the source of light. He sees the morning star*] Oh it is the morning star.

CORPSE: What?

KIBAATE: It is the morning star and I haven't gone home yet.

CORPSE: You haven't done what?

KIBAATE: I haven't gone home yet. After all that boy Damulira may live, oh my bones.

CORPSE: What are you saying?

KIBAATE: What shall I do if Damulira lives?

CORPSE: Which Damulira?

KIBAATE: Oh my head, it is too late now. Damulira may come at any moment.

CORPSE: Which Damulira?

KIBAATE: Damulira is my rival.

CORPSE: Your what?

KIBAATE: My rival.

CORPSE: Your rival?

KIBAATE: Well I will tell you. The diviner warned me not to tell
anybody but I can't keep it secret any longer. Even if I don't say
anything the medicine won't work.

CORPSE: The diviner, the medicine, Damulira? What is all this about?

KIBAATE: I will tell you. My wife is actually much younger than I am.
At one time she was madly in love with Damulira. As a matter of
fact they had arranged to get married, but I interfered. Of course I
loved the girl. What do you expect me to do? She was beautiful and
young, but she didn't love me at all because I was too old for her.
But it didn't matter much to me because Damulira was my employee.
He was the assistant in my shop, a very faithful assistant. My first
aim was to separate him from this girl before they got married. I
packed him off to a friend, who has a shop 400 kilometres away,
then I made approaches to the girl. She refused. I sent expensive
gifts to the parents. Still she refused. I employed one of her brothers
as my assistant and promised to pay fees for the younger brother if
she agreed to marry me. Still she refused. I threatened to stop giving
credit to her parents. This forced her parents to force her to marry
me, although they had hated the idea from the beginning. But she is
rather unhappy with me. She doesn't love me even now and I feel
insecure.

CORPSE: Why don't you let her go? Why do you keep her in captivity?
Do you yourself want to be a captive?

KIBAATE: What do you think I am? I love the woman and I mean to
keep her. I have spent so much money on her. Besides, we have two
children and she is now pregnant.

CORPSE: So what?

KIBAATE: Don't be ridiculous.

CORPSE: What do you mean ridiculous?

KIBAATE: Of course, you realize that she is already a mother and she is
now pregnant, so she can't just go away.

CORPSE: Then what is your worry?

KIBAATE: Damn it, you are just a corpse and you don't understand
human problems.

CORPSE: You will excuse me but I don't see your problem. You want the
woman. You have got the woman you want. You say she can't go
away. Then you continue to worry. What is worrying you?

KIBAATE: There are so many young men who come into the shop and
make eyes at her.

CORPSE: I had thought married people were the happiest and most secure people in the world.

KIBAATE: Moreover yesterday she got a letter from Damulira.

CORPSE: A letter?

KIBAATE: Yes.

CORPSE: You mean she let you read her letter from her boyfriend?

KIBAATE: No she didn't. I found it in her handbag.

CORPSE: What were you doing, searching her handbag? It isn't yours.

KIBAATE: I was curious. With all those young men looking at her, I had to.

CORPSE: But you shouldn't search your wife's handbag.

KIBAATE: Why not? She is my wife. I paid for her and I have a right.

CORPSE: How would you like a woman who searches your brief-case, your pockets, your . . .

KIBAATE: This is different. A woman isn't supposed to search a man's pocket.

CORPSE: Anyway, what did Damulira say in the letter?

KIBAATE: You see he doesn't know that I married the girl. And now he has three months' leave and has written to tell her that he is coming to marry her. And to crown it all, she wrote on the envelope, 'I'm dying to see you. You are my real love . . .'

CORPSE: Now what do you plan to do?

KIBAATE: I am going to bewitch him. That boy must die.

CORPSE: What?

KIBAATE: Damulira must die. The diviner has given me the medicine to kill him.

CORPSE: You told me you love human life.

KIBAATE: Of course I do. I love human life very much but I must safeguard my interests. I love the woman. I can't allow anybody to take her away from me.

CORPSE: Doesn't Damulira love her?

KIBAATE: What does it matter if he loves her? What matters is me. We all love ourselves. We are proud of ourselves. We are selfish. I am a victim of human nature, I can't help it. I'm not ashamed of it and I am not going to hide anything. Damulira must die.

CORPSE: Suppose Damulira also went to a diviner to kill you, or suppose your wife did it?

KIBAATE: Please, please, don't say that!

CORPSE: I was only supposing.

KIBAATE: No . . . no . . .

CORPSE: Do you think the night-dancers are still following us?

KIBAATE: Do you want them to?

CORPSE: Not particularly. I was thinking that we might as well stay here and rest.

Many cocks crow. Kibaate is very nervous.

KIBAATE: What if Damulira doesn't die? What if Damulira comes now? What if my wife runs away with Damulira? Oh my lovely children; their round eyes . . .

CORPSE: Hey mister, the god of the day is beginning to smile. I can see the tip of his tongue over the horizon. I must hide, will you . . .

KIBAATE: How could I know. Nobody can blame me. I behaved in the right way. She is beautiful, and I thought I had . . . Damulira! Oh how could I foresee that you would come back! [*long pause*]

CORPSE [*strongly*]: Tell your relatives to build a shrine for me and perform the ceremony. There won't be peace unless you perform the ceremony.

KIBAATE [*stunned*]: Oh, so you're Damulira. Why didn't you tell me before?

Night-dancers enter with the corpse of Kibaate's wife and walk past Damulira. Kibaate's wife's corpse lingers behind as she talks to Damulira.

KIBAATE'S WIFE: Oh dearest Damulira, is it you really? How did you come here – oh . . . I thought you had given up coming to me.

The night-dancers miss their new corpse and come back for her. They suddenly see the corpse of Damulira.

LEADER OF NIGHT-DANCERS: You Damulira, why were you hiding?

ALL NIGHT-DANCERS: Stop that. Damulira and you are both corpses and we're going to eat you. We order you to walk, and you Damulira, follow her.

KIBAATE [*sobbing for his wife*]: Oh my wife . . . [*a song can be sung at this point, to express mourning*].

Amavi

JACOB HEVI

To my mother Alora and her friend Asikpoe

Some Production Comments

Anyone intending to produce this play should note that
1. there are more than a dozen scenes;
2. the action of the play stretches over twenty years;
3. the two villages of Avegbe Tonu and Agota are separated by a difficult journey;
4. Agota is considered 'foreign'.

Actors will have to show the distance between these two places; and they will also have to give their audience a sense of the passage of time. There are a number of ways that this can be done simply and inexpensively. Here are two suggestions – one for a performance taking place outside in the open air, and the other in a poorly equipped community hall.

An Outside Production of 'Amavi'

For this sort of production you will probably have quite a lot of space. You can arrange your acting areas so that you do not have to change scenes: one stage becomes Avegbe, with Agbeka's house, the yard and the village stream all indicated, and another stage near by becomes Agota. You mark out a 'road' through the audience to connect the two, and this becomes the road along which Amavi travels to reach her new home, and to return to her father. So, instead of changing scenes, the actors themselves move around the whole performance area.

The best sort of platforms would be two areas of raised ground far enough apart for an audience in between them, either sitting on the ground or on chairs or standing, mainly facing the lower of the raised areas which is Avegbe Tonu. The ideal thing would be to have some trees or bushes on the far side of each of the raised areas. If there is only one substantially raised area then that must be Agota: the audience must be given the sense of Agota being high up, because in the end Amavi rolls down the slope which she climbed up with so much determination twenty years earlier as a young bride.

If there is no naturally raised ground where it is most convenient for you to perform the play, then you should set about making some high platform. A truck, for instance, could be camouflaged with grass mats;

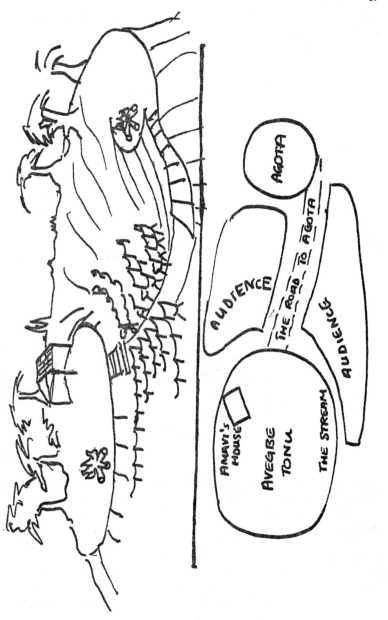

and you could use the roof of the cab to act on, as well as the actual platform of the truck:

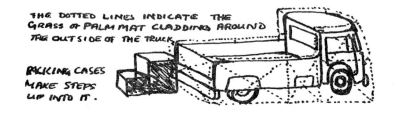

THE DOTTED LINES INDICATE THE GRASS or PALM MAT CLADDING AROUND THE OUTSIDE OF THE TRUCK.

PACKING CASES MAKE STEPS UP INTO IT.

Or you could group together wooden crates of different sizes, and nail some thin strips of wood to the top of the crate to give the outline of Kokutse's house. If you are performing in the grounds of a school or teacher-training college, you could put some desks together – provided your hosts didn't mind! You ought to put canvas or hessian (sacking) over them anyway.

THE DOTTED LINES INDICATE THE OUTLINE IN PLANKS OF KOKUTSE'S HOUSE.

A Performance in a Community Hall

You may have to perform indoors because of the weather, or you may feel that your audience prefers to see a play inside a hall which normally serves as a meeting place for members of the community.

The average church hall or township community hall has a very small stage, and the auditorium floor is usually flat so that the people sitting on the uncomfortable chairs near the back can neither see nor hear very well. The stage is hardly ever well lit; and the curtains marking off the stage can never seem to fulfil their function adequately. It is foolish to try

and fit a play with as many scenes as *Amavi* on to a small stage. If you
did, you would be forever opening and closing the curtains, shifting
scenery and furniture around, and in the end the performance would only
be appreciated by those sitting near the front. You might instead try the
arrangement of stages as suggested for the outside production of the play.
The audience sit facing each other, and the long space between them
becomes the various parts of Avegbe Tonu – the stream, the compound
of Amavi's house and the interior of it. Agota is on the stage, because the
stage is the highest level in the hall. When Kokutse and Amavi climb up
the steep slope, they actually climb – with difficulty – on to the stage.

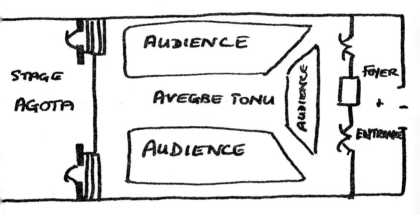

The journey to Agota can be made around the back of the audience
and down one side of the auditorium, then on to the stage. The musicians
can be placed on the front of the stage to one side so that all the action
of the play can be seen clearly. They can therefore more easily integrate
their music with the actors' performance. By having your audience sitting
around the area representing Avegbe Tonu, you will quite naturally
associate the audience with the people of Avegbe. Agota, on the stage
itself, will seem apart and far away. The audience will share with Amavi
the feeling of going far away from home.

How do you show the passage of time? The action of this play takes place
over twenty years. Twenty years is the difference between a bride and a
grandmother, between a father in his prime and an old man, between a
baby and a university student. Actors playing adult characters in this

play will have to change their appearance (clothes, hair, bulk) and their gestures (stooping, slower movements, sadder faces) as the play unfolds.

If there is a reference in the text to, say, Amavi wearing the same cloth after ten years, then the actress playing the part will have to have two pieces of the same cloth, one of which should be artificially faded (by using bleach) and frayed at the seams. If a further reference to the same cloth mentions how dirty it is after her fall, then a third piece of the same cloth must be provided which has been faded and muddied in advance.

The same sort of thing applies to furniture you use. For instance, in order to show Agbeka's chair getting old, you will have to provide at least two chairs, one of which is reasonably new and the other quite clearly beginning to fall to bits. If you are acting the play straight through and are not using curtains, you can substitute the old for the new chair by having Agbeka take his new chair off-stage at the end of one scene and bringing on his old one when the next scene, which takes place several years later, begins.

These comments are starting points. It is important that you share ideas and suggestions amongst the whole group putting on the play during rehearsals. One idea frequently sparks off another, better idea from someone else. The best production springs from the imagination of the group.

Amavi

(*It may be possible to have more than one of these characters played by the same actor.*)

This text sets the action of the play in Ghana. The story begins over twenty years ago, and ends in the present.

SCENE ONE

Before a church in Avegbe Tonu. A priest and a teacher are conversing when a woman passes.

TEACHER [*calling to the woman*]: Amavinọ!

ABRAKPOE [*turning*]: Papa! [*she crosses the stage*]

PRIEST [*seizing the teacher's right arm*]: Ehe-John: I have been thinking to ask you the meaning of these prefixes and suffixes; 'nana', '-nọ', '-tọ' and the rest.

TEACHER: Well. These terms denote parentage, filiation, and status. 'Nana' is an intimate epithet of a child for 'mother'. It is also applied to any woman to show respect. Thus 'nana Adzoa' means 'mother' or 'elderly woman Adzoa', or 'queen mother Adzoa'. In the same way, 'Tọgbui' means 'old man'; it is used for any old man, grandfather, head of a clan or tribe, and chief. In the latter case it is equivalent to 'prince' in English. '-vi' means 'little' in stature or age. Thus, 'Amavi' means 'slim Ama' or 'elder' or 'eldest Ama' in a family, or 'Ama the daughter of Ama'. '-nọ' means 'mother'; thus 'Amavinọ' means 'Amavi's mother'. '-tọ' means 'father'; thus 'Kọdzotọ' means 'Kọdzo's father'. This is the usage.

PRIEST [*nodding his head*]: Ewe is a rich language.

TEACHER [*smiling*]: Yes. It is good that you learn it.

PRIEST: But how can I master all this?

TEACHER: It is very easy. You will get the appropriate meaning from the context and the circumstances in which they are used. From now on be more attentive than you have been so far.

PRIEST [*nodding his head*]: All right, John. I shall be most attentive and inquisitive from now on. [*he looks at his wrist-watch*] John, let us hurry; Amavitọ must be waiting for us by now.

TEACHER [*smiling as the Priest pulls him along*]: He looks so excited about the marriage between his daughter and that young man. [*he looks up into the Priest's face, still smiling*] Father, we are going to taste some 'door knocking wine' today.

The priest and the teacher hurry away to Agbeka's house.

SCENE TWO

Three women meet on the path taken daily by the women of Avegbe Tonu to the pool where the town gets its water. It is the morning gossip time. Agbosi and Adzosi come in carrying pots with the mouths covered with calabashes. They have been talking about something which makes them laugh out loud, almost falling over with their pots. Yawayawae runs in from a different direction trying to catch up with the other two, while balancing her pot on her head and keeping her piece of cloth from falling off.

YAWAYAWAE: My neighbours! I beg you, wait for me too.

ADZOSI [*turning back*]: It is always you for whom we have to wait.
[*she sees Yawayawae's falling cloth*] Look, if you reveal your womanhood to us here now, you will have to kill a sheep. You know you are an old man's wife.

AGBOSI [*also turning and supporting her tilting pot*]: Is that not your Yawayawae?

ADZOSI: Of course. Who else would it be?

YAWAYAWAE [*seeming not to hear her neighbours*]: Good morning.

AGBOSI and ADZOSI [*together*]: Good morning. How are your household?
[*Adzosi turns away, trying to remove something from her toes*].

YAWAYAWAE: They are well.

AGBOSI [*alone*]: How are your children. Are they well?

YAWAYAWAE [*impatiently*]: Eh . . . [*suddenly turning*] Adzosi, you too condescend to respond to my greetings today, at least! Or, are you thinking about your sister's case?

ADZOSI [*still stooping but turning her head to look at Yawayawae*]: But, is that why you are stepping on my toes? What case, anyway?

YAWAYAWAE [*appearing to possess a great secret, and talking with surprise*]:
Oh, I thought you had heard it already. [*all turn to look at her with fresh eagerness. Appearing to be thinking hard she puts her right thumb on her lips*] When was it. Let me see. Ehe – it was, it seems, last Sunday.
[*turning toward Agbosi*] Was it not on Sunday that I came for that kokonte sieve in your house?

AGBOSI: Yes, yes, exactly. I was dressing in my room when I told Tine to give you the sieve.

YAWAYAWAE: It was Sunday, then. I saw Kokutse carrying a pot of palm wine. I was still wondering why Kokutse himself should be sweating under a pot of palm wine that morning. And I was still thinking hard when Nanaga came along. I asked her what it was all about. She told me the palm wine was 'door knocking wine'.

AGBOSI [*pulling her right ear to hear more*]: For what wine? Talk and let me hear. [*opening her mouth in surprise*] That is why Kokutse of all people should bend his neck under a pot of palm wine. I thought . . .

YAWAYAWAE [*cutting in*]: In short, Kokutse is engaged to Amavi.

ADZOSI and AGBOSI: To whom!

YAWAYAWAE: Our only Amavi.

ADZOSI [*opening her mouth and covering it with her right fingers*]: Agbeka and Abrakpoe's Amavi the Great! Anyway, I hope Agbeka will open to him. Aaah! This explains it. These few days Kokutse never passes by my house without a bottle with bubbles spilling over the mouth.

AGBOSI: Eh! It is no joke if there is a wife in the case.

ADZOSI: And he is so excited. Yawayawae, tell us more.

YAWAYAWAE: Atufufue is going to Papadru market today to buy the two tobacco leaves for the full marriage ceremonies on Sunday.

ADZOSI: So soon?

YAWAYAWAE: Yes, it is best they should. For they leave in few days for Agota.

ADZOSI: What '-ta'?

YAWAYAWAE [*shouting into Adzosi's ear*]: Ago-o-taa!

ADZOSI: This sounds like Tamanagu to me: Agbota or Aglota. Agbosi, have you ever heard of such a name?

AGBOSI: If you, a cacao farmer's wife, don't know, do you think I, a corn farmer's wife, know?

YAWAYAWAE: That is the point. We corn farmers only hear such place names 'ho-o-o' like the rushing of a stream. However, I remember Ziava described the place to me last time. Let me see [*a pause*] Aha! He said they said it was somewhere beyond the Amu.

ADZOSI [*suddenly awakening*]: Or, is it Amutome?

YAWAYAWAE [*confidently affirming*]: Yes. There you are. The cacao people.

ADZOSI: Then I have heard about the place. Probably that is the name of the town itself. I know the town has a name different from that of the land; but I just can't keep it in my mind.

YAWAYAWAE: Only you could know it, of course. It is a very vast forest, they say, a jungle.

ADZOSI: Yes, that's it. Its fertility [*clicking her tongue*] is proverbial. There, there is nothing like undergrowth. You have only trees to fell. At night the stars are on the very tops of the giant trees. You would think that you could pluck your cacao just a month after sowing. The people there know nothing about dry season.

AGBOSI: Has your husband been there?

ADZOSI: You see, before we went to Aglame he first tried Amutome. But though the land was excellent, the people were not hospitable at all. If you want to see real witchcraft at work go to Amutome. The natives practise it openly. They even boast of it. An old hag would not be ashamed to tell you that she would be sleeping under you tonight. And truly, you would have to spend the whole night killing snakes under your bed. If they want to pester you, your cacao seedlings would not remain in the soil for a night. They would turn into boars and uproot everything by night. You could see your cutlass fly away from your own hands. And [*touching Agbosi's right shoulder*] do you know, our hut was their meeting ground. We tried to stand them, for some time. But in the long run we were all bedridden, so we left as soon as we could travel.

AGBOSI: Of course, if foreign land is unfavourable, you have to go home.

YAWAYAWAE [*looking very satisfied*]: Adzosi, if I had had an egg I would have broken it on your lips. You really know the place as Atawa described it to me. As she told me, the trees are as tall as the mountains are high.

AGBOSI [*with a little scorn*]: Mountains! Anyway she will soon come back with the hustling, high quality clothes, changing every minute. But first, the mountains, the rains too, and the slippery ground! However, she will soon be back, all smiles.

YAWAYAWAE [*suddenly looking very serious*]: Look, it is not all who comes back with dimples on their cheeks. Some, indeed, come back like gorgeously decked princesses. But others come back as squalid and tattered as myself.

ADZOSI [*putting her right fist to her chin and breathing hard*]: Sister, that is the point. I would willingly be a cacao farmer's wife, but certainly not the one to start the farm. That would be working for the boars to come and enjoy.

YAWAYAWAE: That is true. [*looking down*] But . . . Umm . . . Marriage is like our pottery. If you mould several pots, some will survive the fire and sound [*knocking her pot*] 'gong-gong-gong . . .!' But others will not come out of the fire whole. Some of those which appear very strong will shatter in the fire, and some of those which appear fragile will come out intact. You are never sure which will survive until all are out of the fire. It is all a trial.

ADZOSI: The sun is already overhead. Let us hurry.

All hurry away to the pond with their pots.

SCENE THREE

This scene shows both the inside and outside of Agbeka's house, which is a black rectangular blockhouse with casements on either side of a centre main door. Agbeka is an older man who comes on to the stage and sits in an armchair outside his front door. Two other men, who have come on to the stage with him, are apparently taking their leave of him. They are Kokutse, who hopes to wed Amavi, and Kokutse's father. Abrakpoe, who is Agbeka's wife and the mother of Amavi, is sweeping the front yard with her back to her husband.

AGBEKA [*calling*]: Amavii! [*no response. He turns to Amavi's mother*] Amavinoo! [*Abrakpoe sweeps on for some time without heeding the call. He calls again*] Amavinoo! Or, isn't it you that I am calling?

ABRAKPOE [*heaving herself erect, grumbles to herself as she goes up to Agbeka*]: For what are you calling me?

AGBEKA [*peering into her face, and speaking in a low voice*]: Ke . . . ke . . . ke . . . so you won't even respond to my call. You see [*pressing his two palms on his chest*] whenever you act in that way, you press on my heart. [*he shakes his head*] Very much.

ABRAKPOE [*still standing with her broom*]: Am I not here before you?

AGBEKA [*rising, gathering his cloth around the waist*]: Let us go inside.

Agbeka leading the way, both enter the room. Just after they have gone inside, Amavi, a beautiful, exuberant girl, still in her teens, comes up to the house, carrying a pot of water. She pours the water into a water tank near the house. Inside the room there is a wooden bed with a blanket covering it, and near a window is a table littered with medicine bottles, writing pads and pens.

AGBEKA: Now, Amavino, Amavi's husband . . .

ABRAKPOE [*suddenly becoming wild, but powerless before her husband*]: Since when has Amavi got a husband! [*she turns toward the door as if to leave*].

AGBEKA [*turning to scowl at his wife*]: Ke . . . ke . . . ke . . . Take this from me today: the moment you step out of this room know that you are the sole parent of Amavi! Good or bad [*rubbing his palms one against the other*] my hands, my feet are off her. Do whatever you like with her. You may smear her with pomade and lick her every morning. [*he now clasps his hands, turns to his table and pauses for some time*] The other day I called you here to tell you of the suit, did you say anything to it? You just went out without a word. And were you not here when he brought the palm wine?

ABRAKPOE [*still facing the door*]: Did I take any wine with you? You had been telling me all the time that you were using the bottles of palm wine for medicine. Has the medicine wine turned into 'door knocking wine' today?

AGBEKA [*restraining himself*]: When he brought the pot of palm wine I called you. He delivered the message before you and me: you did not object to it. You just left us, saying you had no time because you were pounding fufu then. In the evening I sent you some. But you said your stomach was not good for palm wine just before bed.

ABRAKPOE [*still facing the door*]: But should people not start working before they marry.

AGBEKA [*becoming heated again*]: Yes, yes; you women. You always want somebody else to work for you. You never want to work for any one. You don't know what this world is. Have you ever seen a baby walking out of the mother's womb? It has to crawl before it walks. [*breathing hard*] You want your daughter to marry a white man's worker. You want her to ride in a 'tonning car'. This is how you women ruin your daughters. So, you are ashamed to have a farmer as your son-in-law. You must be ashamed of me too, then. [*a pause*] Or, you want your daughter to go 'bintu', roaming the streets of the city with her head-gear like this [*demonstrating*] touching the sky.

Abrakpoe supports her chin with her left palm, still facing the door, and blows her nose into her cloth, wiping her face, almost sobbing. She turns to face her husband.

AGBEKA [*standing as if to leave the room, and shaking his stick in her face*]: Go! Find a rich husband for your daughter. But, but woe betide you if you ever refer any case to me.

ABRAKPOE [*gazing on the floor*]: But am I not standing before you still. She is your daughter. Whatever you want to do with her, she is at your disposal.

AGBEKA [*gazes at his wife for some time, then sits down*]: You women. I anticipate your tricks. You think man is a fool. If you think crab's eye is wood, touch it and see.

Both gaze at one another for some time.

ABRAKPOE [*making violent efforts to be calm*]: I beg you to be quick. My cassava is getting overcooked.

AGBEKA [*with a sigh*]: Amavi's husband, Kokutse, has told me that he would like to perform the marriage customs on Sunday. For he leaves with his wife, Amavi, next month for Agota. There he hopes to start a cacao farm.

ABRAKPOE: Is that all?

AGBEKA: Yes, that is all I want to tell you.

ABRAKPOE [*going out, grumbling*]: You do not want your daughter to have a wealthy marriage. You do not want your daughter to be a rich wife. Yet you are drudging night and day to acquire wealth.

AGBEKA [*turning toward the door*]: Amavii!

Amavi, who has been busy outside the house all the while, comes in as Abrakpoe goes out and continues with her sweeping.

AGBEKA [*pointing to the bed*]: Sit down. [*he rests his elbows on the table, thinking hard. Then he spits, and turns towards Amavi.*] Amavi, your husband has just left me. He says you are leaving together next month for his cottage. Because of this matter he is performing your full marriage custom on Sunday. [*Amavi can only gaze at the floor*] Do you hear me?

Amavi wipes her eyes with each hand alternatively, and mumbles vaguely.

AGBEKA [*very sympathetically*]: Amavi, look, if you refuse this offer, you lose your chance for life. An opportunity once lost can never be regained. Chances in life are transitory. [*lowering his head toward her*] Look, listen to this. Do you know Dzamasi – the woman who comes for cocoyam peels every evening? She was the wife of a white man. Unfortunately, the First World War came; her husband was a German, and so he had to escape, leaving her behind, as naked as she had been at birth. You see for yourself what she is now. Not even a dirty farmer [*holding out his cloth*] wants her now. She has to accept even torn clothes from farmers' wives, and she has to beg for food. [*pauses shaking his head*] Amavi, life is not so easy as you think. Look at the earthworm; it has neither eyes nor limbs. Why? It wanted to get all at once. It snatched at them with its mouth and all went down its throat. Now it has to creep on its belly. Full life is attained bit by bit. Do not listen to your playmates; know that genuine wisdom stays only in deaf ears. [*looking into her face and trying to bring forth a smile*]: Daughter, a word to the wise is enough. Go, prepare all that you have, and do whatever he tells you. Respect him; he is your master. He is fully responsible for you. You will come back soon. Cacao does not take much time to produce. Rest is sweetest after labour.

There is some silence.

AMAVI [*still looking at the floor, breaks the silence*]: Thank you.

Amavi leaves the room and goes outside to her mother.

AGBEKA: A first bad step can ruin you for life.

Everyone leaves the stage.

SCENE FOUR

People left the stage at the end of the last scene; and after the musicians have played music to indicate the passage of time, a number of people come back on to the stage: it is straight after the marriage ceremonies of Amavi and Kokutse. Amavi runs into her house crying, but the others don't see this and remain chatting outside the house near the front door.

FIRST WOMAN: Today's ceremonies are the most solemn ceremonies I have ever witnessed in my life.

SECOND WOMAN: Sister. Do you know, the pot of palm wine is yet to be given for my marriage. But I have already had seven children by my husband.

FIRST WOMAN: That is why our husbands do not respect us. Today's ceremonies have really enhanced the image of both families. Everything has been so dazzling: the box, the cloth, the linen, the stool, the kitchen utensils, the two bottles of gin . . . I cannot even remember all. The best of every item. Eh! This is what we call marriage; not the plaything which ours was.

SECOND WOMAN: So is the world. Despite all this the bride does not seem happy.

FIRST WOMAN: The more so I am surprised that she did taste the wine first, before the gathering.

SECOND WOMAN: My friend, could you have refused it against your father's will?

FIRST WOMAN: Of course, I should have known that. This is how our fathers force the yoke on to our necks.

Meanwhile Abrakpoe is in the kitchen area, putting a big pot on the fire. Kofiga, a young man with a goatee beard, enters staggering, trying to dance, to where Abrakpoe is working.

KOFIGA [*bowing, with his hands on his knees, to greet Abrakpoe in the kitchen*]: Good afternoon.

ABRAKPOE [*grinding something in an earthen dish, without raising her head*]: Good morning. [*she continues her work as if she has not noticed Kofiga*]

KOFIGA [*trying to stand erect, and peering at Abrakpoe*]: Amavino, has anything gone wrong today? [*unbuttoning his shirt*] Look, my chest is not strong so I never hide anything in it. The boar says its face is naturally ugly so it never frowns. Or, do you put on such a grave face because of your cassava? Have you forgotten the song [*dancing*] 'No one cooks cassava with a begrudging face. For you know not whether it will be good or not. . . .'

ABRAKPOE [*with a restrained smile*]: Oh Kofiga, you are always making people laugh despite themselves.

KOFIGA [*laughing aloud*]: Oho! Even if you refuse to laugh, your teeth will appear all the same.

All laugh. Amavi goes towards the kitchen.

FIRST WOMAN [*looking at Amavi*]: Oo . . .!

KOFIGA [*suddenly noticing Amavi*]: There she comes, too, with a face as cloudy as Mount Ahato. Ah, she is sobbing. I suppose Papa Agbeka has stepped on your tail this afternoon. You women. That is why you will always lie toward the wall. Now you are weeping for me to see. The season will soon come when the 'money pipa' will be counted in the darkest nook of the room. We shall all see you carry pan loads of yams into your new block house, on your forehead [*he puts his right fist on his forehead and the left on his buttocks and walks around, parodying Amavi carrying the yams*] as if the house were your's. While I shall still be frowning on my bitter cassava in the rugged walls. Anyway, some must marry; some must drink. Those who marry and those who drink are celebrating the same marriage.

All break into laughter.

FIRST WOMAN: Kofiga, don't let air enter my stomach this afternoon. As if he . . .

Kofiga intentionally bangs into her.

SECOND WOMAN [*jumping away from Kofiga*]: Kofiga, why do you not respect women at all?

FIRST WOMAN [*almost falling but trying to push Kofiga away*]: Move away from me! This is the only thing you know.

KOFIGA [*shaking himself*]: She is the choice of my spirits today. Sorry, I have been possessed. Anyway, knowing something foolish is better than knowing nothing at all.

Kofiga dances away.

FIRST WOMAN [*talking to all present*]: Do you think it is easy to marry a beginner in farming? We women are unfortunate by nature.

Several address their words of advice to Amavi.

SECOND WOMAN: Oh, do not cry. It is pitiful but . . .

THIRD WOMAN: That is how we begin, my daughter.

FIRST WOMAN: Do not worry; you will prosper if your fortunes agree.

SECOND WOMAN: Eh! Farmer-husband. [*shaking her head*] And a cacao
farmer! If you say it some may not understand you. You will become
a wretch. A laughing stock!

*Amavi goes into her room. Abrakpoe follows her in. The women outside drift away
from the front door and continue their conversation. In Amavi's bedroom there is a
bare wooden bed near the wall. She starts to pack her few belongings into a big
basin: pieces of cloth, sandals, earthenware. Abrakpoe enters carrying a lantern.*

ABRAKPOE: Amavi.

AMAVI [*turning, in a stifled voice*]: Mami!

ABRAKPOE [*seeming surprised, and pouting her lips*]: Ah! Already packing?
I have not yet heard the first cock-crow. [*she sits on the bare bed*]
Amavi, listen to me very attentively. [*Amavi stops packing*] When you
go away, remember you are a wife. You are no longer a daughter,
so you know all that is involved. If anything happens, there will be
no one to help you. Therefore, obey him. That place is a wilderness.
You have heard all that your father has told you. If you leave your
husband and come back to your father, he will simply not take any
notice of you. [*at this stage Amavi's head droops, and her eyes begin to
water*] Persist. Look, daughter, do not weep. If God wishes, all will
be well. Life is an egg, so handle it with care.

Agbeka enters the room, humming.

AGBEKA: Have you not finished preparing yet? [*he looks into Amavi's face*]
Look, look, look, you are weeping. Stop, stop, stop, those tears
altogether. [*he bows his head towards her*] Daughter, there is no foreign
land. Any place of success is a home. Two to three days and you
will be already used to the place. God willing, you will soon get
your own house and cacao farm. [*he turns to her mother*] Amavino, go
and bring her my kente from under my pillow. [*he gives her something*]
Take this one pound for something on the way.

ABRAKPOE [*having found the kente, and giving it to her husband*]: Here it is.

AGBEKA [*pointing to Amavi*]: Give it to her.

ABRAKPOE [*handing the cloth over to Amavi*]: Here you are. [*he gives her
something in addition*] Take this sixpence for pap on the way.

AMAVI: Thank you.

ABRAKPOE: You know yourself how your hus . . .

Kokutse enters with a gun in a holster, three new cutlasses, and an axe.

KOKUTSE: Agoo! Good morning to you all. [*he puts the things on the floor*]

ABRAKPOE and AGBEKA [*Agbeka shakes hands with Kokutse*]: Good
morning, how is your household?

KǪKUTSE [*very lively*]: They are well. [*he bows*] Togbui.

AGBEKA [*facing Kǫkutse and Amavi*]: Kǫkutse, if you go, care for Amavi
well. You know that you are sister and brother. If there is any
disagreement between you and her, do not be angry. Let no one
hear of it; handle the matter like the catching of a mouse beside a
pot. Amavi is only a child; never quarrel with her, let alone beat
her. Take this from me; the day you beat a woman, you debase
your manhood. That is why I never touch my wife. It is wise to be a
fool before the devil. The tortoise says it cannot run away, so if it
comes to the worst it only retracts its head into its shell. [*shaking his
head*] Do not go about scenting allegations against your wife. Indeed,
many will try to tell you stories about your wife, but turn deaf ears
to them. No one can know your wife better than you, yourself.
Solve all your problems in the privacy of dawn. The people of Agota
are good people. Never provoke anyone; remember, it is wise to be a
fool before a lion. See to what you set out to do. Never look beyond
your boundary. Man must work and sweat. If you stay in your hut
the weeds themselves will come to drive you out. [*suddenly looking
aside as if he has heard something*]

ABRAKPOE: Amavi, if you find that you cannot stay in the hut alone, go
with your husband wherever he goes. To bear the morning dew is
better than to be devoured by a hyena.

KǪKUTSE [*smiling*]: Mother, do not worry. I am strong enough to carry
her wherever I go.

All laugh lightly. A truck's honk is heard outside

AGBEKA: Hurry up now. 'Is this the sort of people they are?' is calling.
[*shaking Kǫkutse's hand*] Soon you will be asking yourself about the
people of Agota; let your natural strength be sufficient for you. If
you hear 'power is here, and power is there' do not move. Our
ancestors have sufficient power to guard you. Amavi, be calm, you
will soon forget about home. God will take you there and bring you
back, safe.

ABRAKPOE: Amavi, you are leaving me now. If your going to the new
place succeeds, it succeeds for all of us. If it fails, it fails all of us.

KǪKUTSE [*his hand still in Agbeka's*]: Thank you for your inspiring words.
I promise to act according to them.

AGBEKA [*still holding his hand*]: The aged say: the ear that hears well is
no basket. My last word is: the comportment of the recipient
determines the worth of the gift.

The second honk is heard outside. All carry the luggage away. The guests who remain on the stage outside Agbeka's house gather around Amavi and Kokutse, as the couple pass between them to the truck; they wish them well. The guests gradually drift away from the acting area. Then Agbeka and Abrakpoe move off. Amavi and Kokutse cross over to the area of the stage which represents the road to Agota.

SCENE FIVE

The Road to Agota – The Chief's House – The Path to Kokutse's House – Kokutse's House.
The young couple are now on the outskirts of Agota. Facing them, far away, are some young men of Agota. Further behind them is a small boy in an oversized pair of shorts shooting his catapult into a tree. The young men peer at the strange travellers. Kokutse wears a pair of thick black boots, khaki trousers, a khaki shirt, and a brown bowler hat; a rifle in a holster hangs from his left shoulder. Amavi, under a heavy load walks behind him.

YOUNG MAN [*suddenly stopping at the sight of the travellers and whispering*]: Look, who is that man! [*he holds a friend's shoulder*] Stop! [*all stop at a loss what to do next*]

KOKUTSE [*talking to Amavi*]: I should think our lorry is now returning home [*glancing at the sun*] we left it on the main road about four hours ago now, you know. [*suddenly he sees the young residents of Agota and walks over to them, raising his hat*] Good afternoon, friends! [*as he approaches, the young men retreat*]

SMALL BOY [*shooting his catapult, he suddenly turns to see the strangers. He looks really frightened and takes to his heels, trying to keep his oversized pair of shorts in place*]: Salifu! Salifu! I am going home!

KOKUTSE [*also shouting to them as he doubles his pace towards them*]: Friends, we want the Chief's house! We mean no harm!

YOUNG MAN [*withdrawing and suddenly turning tail*]: Uuoo!!! Polisi!

The young men and the boy run off confusedly.

KOKUTSE [*turning in disappointment to Amavi who is plodding under her heavy load*]: Amavi, our case is hopeless. These Agota boys take me for a policeman. What are we to do now, Amavi?

Amavi, too exhausted to speak, only heaves a heavy sigh.

KOKUTSE [*still speaking*]: All right, let us rest here. [*he takes the load off*

Amavi's head. Amavi is too weak even to help lift the load down. She wipes her face with a pad. Kokutse takes out a cup from the luggage and hurries away to bring some water. He holds out the cup to her, with an encouraging smile.] Drink the water. [*Amavi gulps the water*] Oh, why didn't you tell me you were tired? We shall reach our land soon. [*taking off his shirt and spreading it out behind her*] Lie down and rest. Maybe an elderly person will come along this time to take us to the Chief. [*soon Amavi is fast asleep*] Kpakpakpi! [*standing arms akimbo, breathing hard and shaking his head*] It has come to the critical point now.

Kokutse shakes himself. He goes away to get the short stump of a tree. He sits on it. Taking off his hat and putting it on his knee he droops his head, supporting it with his palms. He gazes on the ground. After a while, some old men come along. Kokutse hears them talk and he raises his head. He starts up, yawns, and stretches. The men approach him. He stretches out his hand to meet their's, which they proffer very reluctantly.

KOKUTSE: Good afternoon friends.

OLD MAN: Good afternoon, how are you?

KOKUTSE: We are quite well.

OLD MAN: All is peace here.

KOKUTSE: We also are not bringing any bad news. I am Kokutse, the son of Aflamato, from Avegbe Tonu. I have come with my wife, [*pointing to Amavi still sleeping*] and we want to see the Chief of Agota, and also Agbesi who is a farmer here.

OLD MAN: All right, you are welcome. We shall take you to our Chief.

KOKUTSE [*shaking Amavi*]: Amavi, Amavi . . .

OLD MAN [*holding Kokutse's shoulder*]: Papa, your wife is very tired. We shall carry your load. You carry your wife and follow us.

Amavi rises, stretching herself and yawning.

KOKUTSE [*holding her*]: Now we have got some guides willing to take us to the Chief.

ALL THE MEN: Mami, welcome.

AMAVI: Umm . . .

KOKUTSE: Shall I carry you?

AMAVI: No. I can walk [*she staggers along, and Kokutse walks close by her side. All help to carry the luggage.*]

KOKUTSE: We shall soon get to Agbesi's house. There you can rest for some time before we start climbing. [*pointing ahead of them*] The village is somewhere there.

AMAVI [*too tired to be concerned*]: Umm . . .

*They move over to the part of the stage designated as the house of the Chief of Agota.
The Chief, in a smock and a studded skull-cap, sits in an armchair. The Linguist
and the Elders sit beside him in a semicircle. Kokutse and Agbesi and some other
people who have joined them, also sit in the same way, facing the Chief and his
men. Now all stand to exchange handshakes.*

CHIEF: Linguist, are you there. Convey this to our guests: is all peace
here.

LINGUIST: Agbesi, are you there. Convey it to your friends. The Chief
says is all peace here.

AGBESI: Over to you, Kokutse.

KOKUTSE [*standing*]: We also bear no bad news. I am Kokutse, the son
of Aflamato of Avegbe Tonu. My father has told me that he bought
some land from Togbui Mamatala, and he has asked me to come
and start farming it. This is what has brought me and my wife here.
[*he sits down*]

CHIEF: Linguist, tell Agbesi that I have heard all that his friend has
said. I know his father very well. They are welcome.

LINGUIST: Our Chief says, welcome.

AGBESI: Kokutse, well, words need no legs.

KOKUTSE: I thank our Chief very much. My father sends him many
greetings.

CHIEF [*nodding his head*]: Eh . . . Aflamato. I can tell you, he is a very
kind man. Oh, when will he himself come to visit me again? I wish
to see him one of these days. Eh! That man. *They shake hands all
over again. All the others shake hands again also. The hosts put their heads
together and whisper.*

LINGUIST [*standing*]: Have no fear at all. Wait for us, and we shall be
back soon.

*The local people and the Chief leave their seats and go somewhat apart from the
acting area. Agbesi and his friends are left to chat.*

AGBESI: Kokutse, as I see it now, Amavi is too weak to move. I won't
allow you to wreck her on that mountain, so she will stay with me
for a week. Meanwhile you and I will climb the mountain the day
after tomorrow; that will be your first inspection tour.

KOKUTSE: Yes, I have also been thinking about that.

The Chief and Elders return from their conclave.

CHIEF: Linguist – tell our guests that I shall give them a guide to show
them round. He will show them the extent and the limits of the land.

A tall man stands up for all to see.

LINGUIST [*pointing to the tall man*]: This is your guide. In these hands you are safe. Even blindfolded, he can take you all round our land without going a step astray. [*all laugh.*]

KOKUTSE [*to himself*]: With this man combing the darkest nooks of the forests, I wonder whether there is even a rat-hole left for me to dig.

AGBESI [*overhearing him*]: Do not fear; they don't know the art. They can only frighten the animals away. [*speaking aloud to the Chief*]: When will your man be ready?

GUIDE: I am ready at any time.

AGBESI: We would like to go on Saturday.

GUIDE: I am at your service.

Kokutse and Agbesi consult with each other briefly.

AGBESI: Linguist, impart to Togbui that we are pleased with his reception. We would like to turn our backs a little.

CHIEF: Oh! They are free to go.

People all stand and leave the stage. The musicians play to indicate the passage of time. Then Amavi and Kokutse enter and move to that part of the stage representing the steep climb to Kokutse's patch of land. It is a slope with a sheer gradient and there is a flat rock on the right. Amavi is under a heavy load, plodding behind her husband.

KOKUTSE [*pointing at some trees ahead*]: Do you see those trees . . .?

AMAVI: Eh! Still so far away?

KOKUTSE [*turning to look back at her with a smile of reassurance*]: Not at all. Why do you women fear so much? It is just an hour's walk hence.

Amavi shows signs of exhaustion.

KOKUTSE: Not even an hour; it is just behind those trees.

AMAVI [*minding her precarious steps and suddenly crying out*]: Brother Kokutse! [*almost falling with exhaustion, she stops near a slab of rock. She places her hand on it as support. She groans and her whole body gradually droops with the load*]

KOKUTSE [*turning round, runs to her in fear*]: Amavi, what is happening? [*he quickly lifts the load off her head and places it on the slab of rock. He then puts her left arm around his neck, supporting her by the waist. Slowly, he seats her on another rock. He feverishly improvises a cup out of a leaf, and runs for water. He soon brings some water which Amavi gulps down, with a loud yawning sound. Placing his right palm on her heart he asks*] Are you all right now?

AMAVI [*silent for some time and then sobbing*]: Brother, I want to go back home.

KOKUTSE [*taking out a handkerchief to wipe her tears*]: Don't weep, Amavi. We are almost at the end of our journey. [*Amavi becomes a bit calmer. Kokutse stands arms akimbo, looks at the sky, and shaking his head he heaves a heavy sigh. Both gaze at one another.*] Amavi, I won't deceive you. As you see me standing before you now, I haven't even a half-penny on me. I have nothing for transport home. Moreover, if I return home now, I shall have to bear the funeral expenses of Kodzoue who died just after our marriage ceremonies. Amavi [*sitting beside her*] we shall go back home, certainly, but not now.

AMAVI [*after some seconds' silence*]: I want some more water.

Kokutse runs down and soon comes back with a cupful of water. Amavi drinks and staggers to her load. She sits beside it for some time, then she stands up, sighs, and shakes her head. She remakes her pad, and puts it on her head.

KOKUTSE [*placing his hand on the load*]: No, Amavi. I shall carry everything now. [*he tries his best to smile and make her smile, holding out his walking-stick to her*] Have my walking-stick.

Amavi staggers on in front with the stick. Kokutse follows her carrying the load, and they move around the stage, indicating that they are climbing up. Eventually they reach that part of the acting area designated as their farmhouse. At the right is a thatched hut. Two mats of palm leaves are standing against a prop of the shed. A huge, hollow, old tree-stump lies in the middle of the cleared space. It is open at both ends. Amavi arrives at the spot. She sighs, and rests her head on her hands placed atop the walking-stick. She gazes at the ground, immobile. Kokutse puts his load on the stump.

KOKUTSE: Well, here we are. [*he then gets things ready for the night. He brushes out the hollow stump, and he puts essential articles in it. He then brings out a stool he carved. He places it at Amavi's back.*] Sit down and rest. [*he points to the shed and then to the hollow stump*]: We are cooking here and sleeping here. [*Amavi sits down, still gazing at the ground. Kokutse arranges some sticks in the hollow and places a long, palm-leaf mat on them. He then unrolls a thick straw mat over it. He lights a lantern*] Amavi, go inside and rest. Meanwhile I shall prepare some food for you.

AMAVI [*suddenly springing back with a shrill cry*]: Booi!

KOKUTSE: What's the matter! What's the matter!

AMAVI [*pointing to the hollow, trembling*]: A snake!

Kokutse picks up a cassava stick and peers into the hole. He thrashes the stick a few times. He then brings out a dead snake and throws it far into the bush. He ransacks the whole stump, removing everything. He closes one end with a mat and remakes the bed. He beckons Amavi, still trembling far away.]

KOKUTSE: Amavi, it is all over now. Have no fear. Go inside and rest.

Amavi shakes her head. Kokutse looks dejected.

KOKUTSE [*putting his right arm around her waist*]: Then let us go in together. [*He leads her slowly into the hollow. Soon Amavi is fast asleep. Kokutse sneaks out. He stands at the entrance with arms folded.*] Is that I, Kokutse, coming to start a farm? Failure! Curse of nature! Ancestors forbid – oh, my case alone, I know; but somebody's daughter! [*right thumb in his mouth*] Eh! My heart will totter to report what happens, if now something happens, in this strange wilderness. A taste of life's bitterness. [*Whistling for some time, he yawns and sighs. He dozes, nodding his head.*] When . . . I'm so sleepy, too.

He retires into the hollow, blocking the entrance with a mat.
The musicians play at length to indicate the passage of time. Whilst the musicians play, Amavi, Kokutse and other people help to change the scene to indicate the new cottage which Kokutse eventually builds.

SCENE SIX

The main building of the new cottage is an oblong house with mud walls and thatched roof. The kitchen is a hut of thatch, half enclosed with mats. The cottage is surrounded by cacao trees, pawpaw, orange, and palm. At this moment Amavi is preparing 'akple' (a sort of cornflour pudding) in the kitchen. Meanwhile Kokutse comes on to the acting area limping on one leg which is bandaged.

AMAVI [*turning round and suddenly seeing her husband, she jumps up leaving the ladle in the food*]: Ao! What is the matter? Eh! Tell me!

KOKUTSE [*trying to smile*]: Nothing, just a small cut. [*pointing to his left shin, bandaged with plantain leaves sodden with blood*]

AMAVI [*very affectionately*]: Ao! Sorry. [*she brings him a stool*] Sit down here. [*soon she sets before him food and steaming soup. She looks on as her husband gulps everything down*] It is a little overcooked. [*she places her left palm on his right shoulder*] Does it hurt you?

KOKUTSE: Not at all.

AMAVI [*clearing the dishes with unusual agility*]: I shall boil some water for you. [*she runs into the kitchen and gets some hot water in a bucket*] We must dress the wound now.

KOKUTSE: Give me a towel.

Amavi runs into the cottage while Kokutse loosens the binding. Returning with the towel and glancing at the wound she starts, covering her face with her palms.

KOKUTSE [*laughing forcedly*]: Amavi, you women are too timid. This small thing?

AMAVI [*uncovering her face and blushing*]: You are laughing. Is that not the bone?

KOKUTSE [*looking up at her and smiling*]: Not at all. These are only particles of cassava.

AMAVI: But this is a big cut. How has it come about? Tell me.

KOKUTSE: You know, man must look at his blood from time to time. It is only you women who fear blood. [*waving his hand*] Take the things away and bring me a strand of your rug.

Amavi clears things away. She brings him the rug, and Kokutse takes it. She grates some cassava, and pours some Omega oil on it; she gives this to her husband. He puts it on the wound and swathes it with the rug. He sits on the ground, resting his back against the stool. Amavi also sits on another stool, beside him.

AMAVI: Tell me all now.

KOKUTSE: All right. Just as I left you, I knocked my right toe against a stone. You know, it was still not very clear then.

AMAVI: That was a bad omen. Why didn't you return? That is why I tell you to always wait till sunrise. You see for yourself now; you never like to take my advice.

KOKUTSE: What has been done cannot be undone. Something told me 'go back'. But I always like to do some work in the coolness of dawn before the heat of the sun. So I said to myself, 'I must go on. After all I am a man'.

AMAVI: But did you do anything before you cut your leg?

KOKUTSE: Oh, yes. I did something anyway. Do you remember where I was working yesterday while you were roasting cassava?

AMAVI: Ah, yes. I was also working there beside you before I went to set the fire.

KOKUTSE: Exactly. That stony ground; there was a flat rock overgrown with bushes. As I threw the cutlass, it slipped on the flat surface. Before I could check it with my stick it had already reached my shin.

AMAVI: Eh! Didn't it smart!

KǪKUTSE: Not so much. I immediately lopped off a branch of a plantain, and I squeezed some sap into the cut to stop the flow of blood. Luckily I had just uprooted some cassava, and so I scraped a part off with my cutlass. I spread the scrapings over the cut, and then covered it with the blade of the plantain lead, bandaging it together with a strand of plantain fibre.

AMAVI: My sympathies. Anyway, this will make you rest for some time at least.

Amavi and Kǫkutse lean over and comfort each other. The musicians play to indicate the passage of time. Amavi and Kǫkutse drift off the stage and stay there for some moments as the musicians continue to play. When Amavi comes on again she is very pregnant. She emerges, carrying a pot of water from the riverside, supporting her steps with a heavy stick. She pours the water into a big pot, and sits on a stool uneasily.

AMAVI: Why do I feel so heavy today? I should have a nap; that will refresh me. [*she enters a room in the cottage*]

Kǫkutse arrives at the cottage from the farm. In a sack slung over his right shoulder are pieces of bark of medicinal trees. He looks at the empty kitchen, and shakes his head, standing arms akimbo. He calls, but there is no response.

KǪKUTSE: Ah! So Amavi has not yet swept the hearth, and I have to go back to the farm with an empty stomach. In cold and rain I labour; from dawn to dusk, for days and nights I go hunting without food. I feel exceptionally cold today, too. Where has she gone? I have told her never to leave the house without my permission. She is certainly not in Amegbenu's cottage, so far away. Today is Monday, and she knows all are gone to farm. Or . . . [*suddenly, a baby's cry is heard from inside the room. He starts and runs inside*] God! Only God! God help me! [*he comes out of the room with a small bottle of Heineken schnapps and a small glass. He is very excited. He pours some schnapps into the glass, about to pour it into his mouth*] Oh! Yes, I have to give some to the mother first. [*he dashes into the room and comes out soon*] Truly, I know there is God! Oh God, thanks, thanks, thanks a lot! [*he squats to pour libation, placing his skull-cap on his knee, and letting drops of the wine fall to the ground*] All powers of Avegbe, here is your wine. All ancestors of Avegbe, here is your wine. All powers of Tonu, here is your wine. The stool of Tonu, here is your wine. Ancestor Aflamato, here is your wine. Ancestor Akpi, here is your wine. It is nothing evil. You know yourself that man gets livelihood from the bush. Three years ago I also started for the bush with Agbeka's Amavi, your own

daughter. With your help, we arrived here safe and sound. Nine
months ago your daughter became pregnant. I knew you were with
me; I feared nothing. Indeed! You have rewarded my confidence in
you. Now she is with a son. Let me live to see more children,
children's children, and their children fathers and mothers. Let
'Mama's' walls have men to watch over them. Let 'Tǫgbui's' walls
have men to guard them. Guard us and your own son. Give us
wealth and possessions. And give us a safe return home. If anyone
says he will not live nor let us also live, change his mind. If anyone
plays to effect our separation by sowing confusion between us,
confound him. [*he sips the rest of the schnapps*] If . . .

Suddenly Kofiga's voice is heard; he is coming along the path.

KOFIGA: Agoo!

Kǫkutse turns to look along the path.

KOFIGA: Is the owner of the cottage in! Agoo!
KǪKUTSE: Let man come in! [*starting up as Kofiga emerges*] Ko! Or, is it a
  ghost?
KOFIGA [*knocking his chest*]: I, the steam-roller, am on the way. Give way!
  [*he stretches out his hand while still at a distance*] Eh! [*he looks round*] Are you
  people planting the cacao or you are only taming wild cacao forest?
  [*he covers his mouth*] Three years' cacao! [*he stands dumbfounded for some
  time, and then notices the glass and bottle*] I see you are on something.
  Finish it off at once. Or . . .
KǪKUTSE [*spitting out the wine from his mouth*]: Fie!
KOFIGA: Dafe!
KǪKUTSE: Yeako! [*putting the bottle and glass away*] Eh! Eh! Eh!!!
BOTH [*embracing very excitedly*]: Atoo!
KOFIGA: Good news or bad news?
KǪKUTSE: More than good news. [*slapping his palm against that of Kofiga*]
  You are a bearer of good fortune.
KOFIGA: I am happy about that. Where is Amavi, first of all.
KǪKUTSE [*dashing into the kitchen*]: I have not yet given you water. [*he
  brings him a cup of water, sipping a little before giving it to Kofiga*]
KOFIGA [*having gulped the water, dashes into the kitchen himself*]: I am in my
  own house. I'll get some more water myself.
KǪKUTSE [*still shaking Kofiga's hand*]: Before I tell you where Amavi is
  let us enter the room. [*pulling him along*] I have something for you.
KOFIGA [*exclaiming*]: What! Have you killed an elephant?

They enter the room. Kofiga's cries of astonishment echo outside.

KOFIGA: Bobobo! Amavi! Oh! [*clapping*] You have already broken down the anthill. Truly! There is God! I am truly a man of good omen. The feet are suited to climbing. Look at the head; fitting exactly the cocao basket. [*laughter within*]

Kofiga and Kokutse come out.

KOFIGA: Let us see to the hot water and soup before we continue our greetings.

KOKUTSE: The soup needs only heating. But let me put some water on the fire.

Kokutse enters the kitchen. He soon comes out with a stool and sits beside Kofiga.

KOKUTSE: Shake my hand once more. [*they shake hands*] That is Kofiga himself. I have heard of your coming; but never thought you would come so soon. [*still holding his hand*]

KOFIGA: I am on the way.

KOKUTSE: Who has brought you all the way here?

KOFIGA: You know us, old men. We have only to pronounce a word and we are wherever we want to be.

KOKUTSE: That's it. Have my hand once more, man.

KOFIGA: A young man of Agota brought me to Amegbenu's cottage last Thursday; and one of Amegbenu's labourers who was going to Kedzi brought me as far as the entrance of your cottage. And, so, here I am.

KOKUTSE: Why couldn't you come to us at once?

KOFIGA: My brother, your mountain forbade it. If I had dared attempt it you would have been carrying a corpse to Avegbe by now. When I arrived at Amegbenu's cottage I was simply a mangled heap of bones and flesh; I was really crawling on my knees. Your mountain really challenged my manhood. But for the shame of it I would have returned home and told my father that Agota spirits didn't allow me passage.

KOKUTSE: Anyway, I am happy you are here at last. You know, Amavi is not so feminine as she seems. She climbed almost to the top with her heavy load. She refused my help until she became thoroughly exhausted. Eh! She made me tremble that day.

KOFIGA: Tell me again. Do you say Amavi came half-way up this sheer slope? Then I should be ashamed of myself.

KOKUTSE: More than half-way – almost all the way.

KOFIGA [*in a very low voice*]: Lucky to have such a partner. I should think she can throw her arm too.

KQKUTSE: Believe it or not, we work abreast. Kofiga, my father has always told me to be careful about women, but, I can say that Amavi forestalls my doubts. She makes mistakes occasionally, but whenever I remember our first night here, my heart cools down, and I curse myself for having taken offence at all.

KOFIGA: Kqkutse, I won't deceive you; marriage is a practical study in human relationships.

KQKUTSE: Do you see the results of my three years' efforts?

KOFIGA [*looking round and nodding*]: I am at my wits' end to see real pods on your cacao. Anyway, I have come too; we shall see.

KQKUTSE: I know you. You will soon become the Chief of Agota itself.

KOFIGA: You wait. Give me three months and I shall be master over the whole Amutome. [*gesticulating*] You will no longer get your monkeys. For those, our ancestors, I am fully prepared. We shall be swinging on the lianas and branches together. All your animals will be attracted into my traps. Lastly, your cacao will have to wait for mine. [*a moment's silence*] Kqkutse, I have a secret to tell you. Have you come across the white man's new cacao seeds yet? I mean the type they grow in their country?

KQKUTSE: How could I hear about such a thing in the bush here? Tell me, my friend.

KOFIGA: It is all very easy. You have only to go to Agota. UAC . . .

KQKUTSE: Ptchaw! Kofiga, is it not Amutome Kingsway rather?

KOFIGA: Not at all [*looking serious*] You just go to Agota UAC, and ask for the white man's cacao beans. Buy a tin of them, roast all black. Go and bury all of them in the centre of your farm, then come back home and sleep for six months.

KQKUTSE: No weeds?

KOFIGA: Not at all. Within six months your cacao pods are already ripe. This is the type I am going to plant.

KQKUTSE [*almost falling over with laughter*]: Kofiga, there is no end to your jokes. Anyway, take this from me; if you dare tell your labourers this they will one day roast all your cacao seeds for the nursery.

KOFIGA: That will be very wise of them. [*Both laugh aloud*] Kqkutse, I must be going. The marks on the palm are becoming indistinct. I don't want to walk on my mouth back to my host's house.

KQKUTSE: Why not come to stay here.

KOFIGA: Don't worry. I have come. [*standing*] I am not just passing by. Let me go and bid Amavi good-bye.

Amavi emerges from the room, her stomach tied with an old headkerchief.

AMAVI: Fo Kofiga, won't you stay here for the night?

KOFIGA [*turning, mouth wide open*]: Eh! Amavi! On what kind of animal
do you people feed to have such extraordinary strength? Already out
of bed! Kọkutse, as I see it, I am no match for you and your wife.
Anyway, Amavi, be sure that you and I will never work abreast on
the farm, otherwise you will disgrace a bearded man like myself.
Amavi, next time will do. I hope to be here on the eighth day for
the outdooring ceremonies.

AMAVI: Yoo! Convey my greetings to Amegbenu and Kofinọ for me,
and don't forget to deliver the good news. Tell them that God has
delivered me out of it at last.

KOFIGA: You need not tell me that. You know me. I am the herald. I
deliver even unsanctioned messages. When will you go to show little
Kọdzo to our people at home. How happy they will be to see your
healthy child.

Amavi and Kọkutse see Kofiga off. Amavi lags behind.

KỌKUTSE: I have been thinking of it. I think we should go home as soon
as possible.

KOFIGA: Kọkutse, playing apart, I have heard your praises of your wife.
Let me tell you this. I have heard many such eulogies which fail in the
long run. The greater the attachment, the more frivolous and
unreasonable the cause of separation. Man's mind is a clock; it
changes at the least tick. I am happy that you are both happy.
You know me. [*holding his ribs*] My ribs are very light, so I never
keep anything in my heart. Before I came here, I knew more about
the women of Agota than the natives themselves. They can turn you
upside down; they can turn your head against your own wife at any
time. Kọkutse, listen well. The day you allow any woman of Agota
to influence you, you are doomed!

Kọkutse, Kofiga and Amavi go off the stage. The musicians play.

SCENE SEVEN

*The scene has moved back to Avegbe Tonu, and Agbeka's house; it is two years
later. There is no radical change in the setting. The armchair is still at the entrance.
Agbeka is quaking his thighs with a piece of cloth around his waist. Abrakpoe is
busy in the kitchen. A girl runs into the house.*

GIRL: Nana! Nana! Sister Amavi is back. She has just come down from the lorry.

ABRAKPOE [*excited*]: Ao! My daughter is back home. Amavito, I have been saying this just now. That is why fowls have been fighting in the house.

She runs to embrace Amavi who enters the house; a girl is carrying little Kodzo who is two years old. Other children struggle to get to him, and to surround Amavi.

ABRAKPOE: Atoo! My only Amavi. My only daughter. Is that your face?

AGBEKA [*getting up for a stool*]: Kwami, bring her some water! Some roasted cornflour! [*a boy stands by and a girl runs into the kitchen. They give him a calabash of cornflour and water. He mixes the flour in the water, and pours it on the ground. Amavi steps in it, and then puts Kodzo's right foot in it also. Amavi now sits on a stool beside her father. Other children and some women surround them*] Give me Togbui's child. [*receiving the child in his arms*] What is it, anyway?

AMAVI: He is Kodzo.

AGBEKA: Togbui's own Kodzo! [*he throws him into the air several times*] I should think he is shooting 'gon' already. Aflamato told me the other day that he had already bought a 'double bar' for him. Kodzo, how old are you?

AMAVI: Two years.

AGBEKA: We have even forgotten our greetings.

AMAVI: Good evening.

AGBEKA: Good evening. How are the people there.

AMAVI: They are well.

AGBEKA: The Chief, Linguist, Amegbenu, and my Kofiga too.

AMAVI: They send you greetings.

AGBEKA: Kofiga arrived safely?

AMAVI: Yes. He came to us the very day Kodzo was born. He made us laugh our heads off before he left us.

AGBEKA: I should think he is the Chief of Agota by now.

AMAVI: That is obvious. He is a friend to every resident. Wherever you are you can always hear the echo of singing or whistling. He is always in high spirits.

AGBEKA: Good. Here all is peace.

AMAVI: We have also brought no bad news. We had been planning to come for some time but many a time Kodzo's father postponed it. Last Sunday night he told me I should prepare for I would be coming home the following Tuesday. He could not come himself because his new farm is still to be cleared by labourers some time next week. So I got my few things ready; and here I am.

ABRAKPOE: You are welcome.

AMAVI: Thank you.

ABRAKPOE: How is your husband?

AMAVI: He greets you.

ABRAKPOE: How are your people there?

AMAVI: They are well.

ABRAKPOE [*putting her right hand to her chin*]: Amavi [*she flings out her arms. looking at the child*] Mama's son. [*the child struggles out of Agbeka's hands to embrace his grandmother*] Mama's son. Atooo!

AMAVI: Kọdzo, you are now in town; no longer in the cottage. [*taking him from his grandmother*] Look, Kọdzo [*pointing to Agbeka*] this is Tata. Say it: Ta . . . ta. . . .

KỌDZO [*mumbling*]: Ta . . . t . . . ta . . .

AMAVI: Taa . . . ta.

KỌDZO: Taa . . . ta.

AMAVI [*turning to Abrakpoe*]: This is Mama. Say it.

KỌDZO: Mam . . . ma.

AMAVI: Mama.

KỌDZO: Ma . . . ma.

AMAVI: Papa, I would like to go and greet my in-laws too.

AGBEKA: Certainly you must go.

Amavi stands and leaves. The children follow her out of the house.

AGBEKA: Amavinọ, do you see for yourself now? I told you that all would be well. You nearly ruined Amavi's life – naturally a daughter must marry.

ABRAKPOE: Amavitọ, I have been with you for over twenty years now. Amavi has been married for only five years now, and five years are too short to decide anything.

AGBEKA: You women! For me, five years is long enough to decide everything.

ABRAKPOE [*in a low voice*]: Has he sent you anything?

AGBEKA: There you go again. You women! Always with palms open for something. You never give yourselves. Anyway have you searched through her luggage?

ABRAKPOE: For my part, I have still to see whether this marriage is a success. Is she not using the kente you gave her to carry her first child? [*walking away*] I hope it is successful. But all the same, it has yet to be proved. Even if I die, I shall know the news in the grave.

Musicians play and the scene shifts to that part of the stage which represents the path to the pond. Some women have come on chattering and laughing.

FIRST WOMAN: Why has she come back at all?

SECOND WOMAN: Haven't you heard about it? Then you are outside the town of Tonu.

FIRST WOMAN: You see. We don't hear anything at our Zongo. We shall be overrun one day by enemy forces before we get to know of an invasion.

SECOND WOMAN: She returned with a son, but without the husband. I think it was about a week ago.

FIRST WOMAN: Without her husband?

SECOND WOMAN: Yes.

FIRST WOMAN: Has something happened, or . . .?

SECOND WOMAN: Probably. I happened to pass by her father's house when she arrived. There were many people around when she delivered her message . . . I did not hear it clearly but it seems Kofiga and the husband have not been on good terms of late, so the husband sent her home.

THIRD WOMAN: I was in her father-in-law's house when she went there. The whole town was her retinue. How happy the old man was; he poured libation immediately. She said her husband had sent her to show their first-born to his father. She did not mention any quarrels, anyway.

SECOND WOMAN: That was what I heard anyway.

FIRST WOMAN: How could Kofiga of all people quarrel with any one at all? Let alone with his crony, Kokutse. How is their cacao doing in that land of witches?

THIRD WOMAN: She said her husband had already sold about ten loads.

SECOND WOMAN: Ten loads! Why, then, does she wear such faded clothes, just like one of us!

THIRD WOMAN: And her head-gear too! I think she is used to cottage life; she is now used to the dirty part of the work.

SECOND WOMAN: But she has turned so virile!

THIRD WOMAN: My friend, throwing a cutlass at thick trees and lianas, and climbing mountains with a load almost every day is no feminine task.

SECOND WOMAN: She has become lean too. She is now real 'Amavi', almost the size of this thin arm of mine. Five years ago she was 'Amaga', she was so stout.

Musicians play. As they complete their activities, all the women leave.

SCENE EIGHT

Back at Kọkutse's cottage. It is a few years later. There are some palm, orange, and cacao trees around – various things to indicate that the farm has some prosperity. Kọkutse enters, having just returned from night-hunting. He is soaked with rain and shivering. He lays down his hunting kit in front of the door.

KỌKUTSE: Today's cold has really numbed my very bones. And these days, no animals at all. My traps lie untouched. Is this the sort of life I have set out to lead? And my head aches too – they say there are witches. Is it death or life? Bad reasons! Amavi too, since her first child she has not been as obedient to me as she used to be before. How do they fare at home now? the third visit without me. I must change these clothes. [*he sits near the fire*]

Torogbani, an old woman, enters quietly.

TOROGBANI [*suddenly cries*]: Ago! Ago! Ago!

KỌKUTSE [*turning his neck and seeing the woman*]: This diviness again, pestering my life! She will not let me think for myself. Amavi is in Avegbe, so she has come here once again. So timely! Terrible! Ame! Oh, Mami Torogbani, welcome [*trying to compose himself*]

The woman draws a stool near him. She is holding a wrapped headkerchief.

TOROGBANI: Papa, where is your wife?

KỌKUTSE: She has gone home with the small children. She is to return with the school pupils for holidays.

TOROGBANI: Yes, that is true. This is her third visit without you. I see all, Papa, I see all.

KỌKUTSE: Let me give you some water.

TOROGBANI: Water is not necessary, Papa. [*a pause*] Papa Kọkutse, that city girl greets you.

KỌKUTSE [*a bit bewildered*]: Which girl?

TOROGBANI [*smiling*]: Oh . . . my niece. The one who brings you your meals when you are in town for cacao meetings.

KỌKUTSE: Aha! [*with a dry smile*] Eh! [*suddenly holding his head*] My head. [*he rests his head on his thighs for some time*]

TOROGBANI: Papa, something for you. [*she loosens the headkerchief, but suddenly stops*] How is your cacao?

KỌKUTSE [*in a muffled voice while peering at the wrapping on the ground*]: My cacao? [*a pause*] It is on.

TOROGBANI: I see. It is not doing well these days. Let me see. [*she unwraps the headkerchief. In it are fine sand and some cowries. She throws the cowries three times on the sand.*] Why? Somebody else's cacao is doing very well while your's is rotting on the tree. But you came long before him. I see also that you are not well. Agota is not a good village at all. There are bad spirits. Let me see. [*she throws the cowries again three times, shaking her head*] I see all. I see everything. Papa. Be careful. Whenever I come to you know that I have seen something. Take note of the witch-birds. You are very kind. So I tell you everything.

Kofiga's voice, singing, echos in the distance.

TOROGBANI [*wrapping up her things in haste*]: Papa, I am going. I shall tell you more when you come to town. Sewa will come for some cassava tomorrow.

Torogbani hurries away. Kofiga's voice becomes louder and louder, and he enters slowly, swaying from side to de.

KOFIGA: Ago-o! no human being in the hut?

KOKUTSE: Ame!

KOFIGA: Ao! Ao! [*suddenly notices the woman now vanishing among the cacao trees.*] Kokutse! A bachelor! Cooking? You will die, hein! Just come in from hunting, I suppose. Before I sit down, tell me who has just left you?

KOKUTSE: An old woman has just passed by.

KOFIGA: I never knew your compound was a highway. I admit everything is dancing before me, but I say I recognize the back of that . . . in short, I saw Mami Torogbani. However, don't mind that. Tell me. Zukpe!

KOKUTSE [*responding reluctantly*]: Zukpe!

KOFIGA: You are a bachelor. Why do you go to farm with an empty stomach and stay there until night? And your night hunting expeditions too, when most often you get nothing. Anyway, if you die we shall drink over your head. But I have no time to carry a corpse from Agota to Avegbe Tonu these days. Again, I never hide anything in my life. Beware of the women of Agota, especially their old hags. [*turning to go*] Zukpe, I am going.

KOKUTSE: Stay with me for some time.

KOFIGA: No. I am going [*tottering away*]

KOKUTSE: Zukpe! I am calling you.

KOFIGA: White men say 'bye-bye!' You are ill. I have to go and ask my daughter Afua to come and stay with you until your wife comes back.

Kofiga exits, and his song dies in the distance.

KƆKUTSE [*standing and stretching himself with a sigh*]: Eh! 'Kpakpakpi!'
This woman. Let me see. First, my cacao. Yes, since Kofiga's arrival
my cacao has not been doing well. And his . . . he sold a hundred
loads last year. And mine . . . only ninety. But my farm is far larger
than his. But Kofiga! I know him well. Ah yes, he told me something
the day he stepped into my cottage. That was the first time: he said
'Anyway, I have come too; we shall see!' But that was just a joke.
My head! Yes, these witch-birds. They will not let me sleep. Yes,
yes. Their noise increases when Amavi is away.

Afua, a girl in her early teens enters, carrying a bucket of hot water.

AFUA: Agoo!
KƆKUTSE [*turning his head*]: Eh! Afua. Has your father reached home
already? I should think he is flying today.

*Afua busies herself preparing a hot bath for Kokutse, who continues to sit by the
fire as the musicians start to play to indicate the passage of time. As they play,
people come on to the stage and help Kokutse build his new cottage which is much
larger than the first one. Amavi has returned, and is sweeping the compound when
Afua comes on again. The musicians stop playing as Amavi speaks.*

AMAVI [*sweeping and suddenly catching sight of Afua*]: Eh! Afua! [*standing erect,
and twiddling her broom*] Since I came back from home this is the
only time that you have come to greet me.
AFUA [*coyly*]: Oh, I am sorry.
AMAVI: Nevertheless, I thank you for having done my work while I was
away. I have learnt you were attending your father while he was ill.
AFUA: Don't mention it at all.
AMAVI [*getting near her and talking in a low voice*]: Afua, tell me. Did you
also see those headkerchiefs on Kodzoto's bed?
AFUA: Yes, I saw them the other day when I entered the room for a
towel. I suppose they belong to Sewa.
AMAVI [*trying to suppress her surprise*]: Which Sewa?
AFUA: A certain girl from Agota. She came here often for cassava when
you were away. She had been buying sugar and salt from Kodzoto.
AMAVI [*nodding her head*]: But why are they on the bed and nowhere else?
AFUA [*looking away and mumbling*]: I too, can't tell.
AMAVI: Of course, you are not the right person to answer this question.
I should think you came for something.
AFUA: Yes, I left our big pot here last Sunday.

AMAVI: I saw it under the eaves. See whether you can find it in the kitchen. [*Afua goes towards the kitchen*] Is it there?

AFUA: I have not seen it yet.

AMAVI: Then . . .

AFUA: Yes, here it is. [*she comes out*] Thank you.

AMAVI: Thanking me. I, rather, should thank you, my daughter. You have done your very best.

AFUA [*turning to go*]: Ko̱dzono̱, please I am going.

AMAVI: All right. Greet your mother and your sisters and brothers for me. Ask your mother whether she has got anything for Agota market next Monday.

Afua leaves.

AMAVI: That is why Ko̱kutse has been staying so long in town these days. He seems to have committee meetings almost every day. And my husband goes and comes back only after two, three, and sometimes, four whole days. Whenever I query him it is either 'the meeting lasted far into the night' or 'a clerk came to audit the accounts'. Deceiving me; after twenty years of marriage! Not me [*she spits and beats her breast*] Himself! God is my judge. I have nothing to say.

Amavi turns round and her eyes meet her husband leading a young woman. She appears to be more a girl than a woman. She is carrying a big handbag. Folded pieces of cloth jut out through the zip opening.

AMAVI: Eh! Ko̱dzoto̱, who is this . . .?

KO̱KUTSE [*in a rough voice*]: She is my wife.

Amavi turns away and continues her work as if nothing has happened. The children – if the producer is able to have any on the stage about Amavi – keep on staring at their father and the lady. Not one of them makes any attempt to welcome his father.

KO̱KUTSE [*sitting on a rock in the centre of the house and taking off his shoes*]: Kwami!

KWAMI [*one of his sons*]: Papa!

KO̱KUTSE: Why are you all gazing at me like bulls. Can't you give me water? Or you don't see the guest standing? [*Kwami brings him a cup of water*] Not me. Give it to Sewa. [*Kwami first looks round, a bit confused*] Or, you don't hear me?

KWAMI [*looking at the young woman gives the water to her. He waits to take the cup back*]: Shall I bring you more?

KO̱KUTSE [*suddenly turning on Kwami*]: Is that what you are taught at

school? [*shouting*] Run and bring me some too! Quick! [*Kwami runs
for the water. Meanwhile Amavi has finished her work*] Kǫdzonǫ!

AMAVI: Papa! [*she hurries up to him and stands before him*]

KǪKUTSE: Remove your things to the empty room near the children's.
[*he turns toward Sewa*] Sewa, take your things into my room.

*Amavi gazes at him, dumbfounded for some time. Musicians play furiously. Time
passes. People go into the house, tense and angry. As the music ends Kǫkutse comes
out of his house ready for work, in a new smock. A sack dangles from his shoulder.
There are some seedlings of cacao and oranges in it. Sewa comes out of the house
too, dragging her feet on the ground.*

SEWA [*with a clumsy smile*]: Brother Kǫkutse.

KǪKUTSE: Sewa, what is the matter? [*he swats an insect on his calf with the
flat of his cutlass*]

SEWA [*with simulated coyness, wriggling herself*]: I would like to pay a visit
to my aunt. It is a long time since I saw her.

KǪKUTSE: Yes, yes, Torogbani, the diviness. It is high time I visited her
myself too. You may go. But don't bring back any bad augury, hein?

SEWA: All right, thank you, Brother Kǫkutse.

*She wraps her cloth round herself, leaving only her face showing. She then shuffles
back into her bedroom.*

*As Kǫkutse turns to go he knocks his right toe against a stone. He starts, suddenly
raising his foot. He puts down his sack near the stone. He goes back into his room,
coming out with a small bottle of schnapps and a small glass. At that very moment
Amavi comes in with a pot of water. As she passes by the stone and turns to look
at the sack a drop of water falls on the stone. Kǫkutse turns and scowls at her. He
steps forward and takes off his skull-cap. He fills the glass with some schnapps. He
now lest drops fall on to the stone.*

KǪKUTSE: All ancestors, here is your wine. All ancestor-stools, here is
your wine. You know that I am in a foreign land. I have come here
in search of wealth which I can take home. If any power or any
man thwarts my plans it is only you who know it. If anybody wishes
me evil, let it recoil on his or her own head. If anyone will not live
and let me live, see to him yourselves. If it is in my own house, reveal
it. Let the way be clear for me . . . kusekusekuse'. *He sips the rest of
the wine, pours out the dregs of the glass, and spits it out of his mouth. He
returns the glass and bottle to his bedroom and comes out again. Amavi enters.*

AMAVI: Kǫdzotǫ, please, for about a week now I have not been feeling
well. My head is almost falling to the ground; here, here, and
everywhere. I . . .

KOKUTSE: You had better tell me what you want. I am in a hurry. I
    am not so free as you women. You are never healthy [*he turns to go*]

AMAVI: Ao! So you won't listen to me, Brother Kokutse.

KOKUTSE [*turning towards her*]: Tell me what you want to tell me. Don't
    provoke me this morning; I have not yet tasted salt.

AMAVI: I beg you . . .

KOKUTSE: I have heard that.

AMAVI: Kindly ask your wife to help me, at least today. There is so
    much to be done in the house, but your wife always sleeps till the
    sun is overhead. After fetching water there is the meal to be
    prepared, clothes to be washed, and the house to be swept, and I
    have to do all alone. Oh, I shall die with all this.

KOKUTSE [*shaking his right index finger in Amavi's face*]: I don't want to
    talk this morning, so be careful not to arouse my anger.

AMAVI [*throwing back her head to avoid the threatening finger*]: What have I
    done? Kodzoto, what have I done.

KOKUTSE: Let me tell you. I . . . I . . . I married you. And I . . . I . . . I
    chose to marry Sewa too. That does not concern you. Let me tell
    you that I am not a child. Though my hair is not yet grey I know
    you women. I know your evil machinations. You women! Hear this
    once and for all; if you play with me, you will be sorry. You will see
    it all in the flicker of a second like a picture on a cinema screen.

*Amavi, almost sobbing, looks downwards, trying to support her chin with her left
hand. In doing so she lets the pot fall into the water in the tank.*

KOKUTSE [*ablaze with wrath*]: How dare you pour water on that stone!
    The ancestors are always guarding my footsteps. I, Aflamato's
    Kokutse, have not come to this wilderness empty handed. If you
    don't know, know it today. I can hear things; I can see things. How
    dare you pour water on that stone? [*points to the stone against which he
    knocked his toe*] With all this space, that is the only place you chose to
    pass with your water. Look, don't trouble me, don't, don't!

*He suddenly turns his back on Amavi, puts on his cap, picks up his sack and
cutlass, and vanishes among the cacao trees.*

AMAVI: Ao! Is it all come to this? Always the same unnecessary rage
    whenever he comes back from town and I utter a word to him.
    [*placing her palms on her breast*] Is this I, the Saturday born? Is this
    the daughter of Agbeka? Who asked me . . .?

A voice is heard. Kofiga enters.

KOFIGA [*singing aloud*]:

> *Ao, ao, the day of my death which I don't know.*
> *What pains me is that I don't know the day of my death . . .*

[An appropriate song in your own local language may be used.]

AMAVI: Eh! Kofiga is coming once again.

KOFIGA [*in a drunken voice, approaches Amavi, trying to be steady, but still swaying; he looks up at her, squinting*]: Ao, ao . . . But where is your face going this morning? It appears too long, I am afraid.

AMAVI [*trying to smile but producing only a frown*]: Eh! Kofiga, I can see you have doused your beard in the calabash this morning already.

KOFIGA [*reeling away with a droll burlesque of a dance, he brings out a small drum from Kokutse's kitchen, drumming and dancing around*]: I am Akpi himself! Where are your body-guards?

AMAVI: They are gone to inspect their traps.

KOFIGA: Anyway, good morning.

AMAVI: Good morning, how are your household?

KOFIGA: They are singing their heads off by now. Don't you hear them from here. Where is your husband?

AMAVI: Asking about Kokutse in the house this daylight?

KOFIGA: Of course, I shouldn't have asked that this noon. Eh! What a man of double strength. Never met a man so agile; able to endure anything, rain, sun, light, darkness, and all things. He can do without sleep for days on end. When did he return from hunting yesterday?

AMAVI: Do I know? I saw him only this morning, and he has not taken any food at all today.

KOFIGA: Probably since yesterday. Yet he is off once again, enduring the morning cold and dew. Tell him, if he happens to come back before tomorrow morning, that I am not strong enough to carry any corpse down this Agota scarp to Avegbe. [*with a graphic demonstration of plodding under a heavy load down a slope*] Anyway, he has white ants at home, who will converge on the fruits of his self-denial when he is no more. I for one, I am only concerned with what I can get today and leave some for my children tomorrow. For the rest Kofiga is satisfied, in and out, as long as he gets his calabash of palm wine every morning. I don't want any witch to put onion into her eyes, deceiving herself that she is weeping over my premature death [*a pause. Suddenly looking back*] Where is your lady?

AMAVI: Go and knock.

KOFIGA: Do you mean she is still in bed?

AMAVI: You knock and see for yourself.

KOFIGA [*knocking*]: Kokutse's Queen! [*pressing his right ear on the door*] Aha! I hear her movement. She is wriggling herself like a rat in a hole when the smoke is pumped into it. Mami Goro! Morning! What a wife! I am told she is a schoolgirl.

AMAVI: But what do you think? They even speak the white man's language sometimes.

KOFIGA: I can see your husband is not joking at all. But has he ever sat at a desk?

AMAVI: Who knows? Probably they do that only to tease me, as I am only an illiterate.

KOFIGA: That is why Kokutse of all people does not face me these days. I suppose he has been advised by his city lady to shun us poor villagers. Nevertheless, Amavi, don't worry. The thief can never get more than the farmer.

AMAVI: But, do you know who is the farmer in this case?

KOFIGA: Amavi, don't fear any overthrow. What! Under the very eyes of the youths of Avegbe. That is impossible. If you see any sign, cry 'Ootoo . . .' We will be here at once. See, the home spirit has entered me already.

He dances off.
Kokutse suddenly emerges from behind a corner of the cottage, soaked by the morning dew.

KOKUTSE: Amavi, what is the matter in my house? Anything here for me to eat?

AMAVI [*composed*]: It is your Kofiga. [*trying to smile*] The one who is constantly wet.

KOKUTSE: But, what is he doing in my house every morning? [*Amavi simply gazes at him. He also gazes at the ground, with pursed lips for some time, blurting out*] Of course you wouldn't know.

He goes into his room, comes out with a hunter's lamp, and exits.

AMAVI [*gazing at his back*]: Kodzoto, where are you going? [*she tries to say something but the words stick in her throat. She shakes her head. She sits on a slab of rock near the water-tank, supporting her chin on her left palm, still mumbling some words. Suddenly she rises*] What fate has brought me here? And my rival too. She won't do a thing in the house. Since her arrival in this house she has never even picked up a strand of broom to make a streak on the ground. She does not know even how to grind pepper; I have to teach her. And yet my husband does not see that. I fear only for my children. What will become of them when I am no longer with them? Kokutse's Queen! I shall arouse her now. It is too much for me to bear. [*she knocks several times at the door*] Sewa! Sewa! The sun is already right overhead.

A sigh is heard. Then the door gradually opens, revealing Sewa's clouded, sleepy face.

SEWA: Who is troubling me here?

The voices of men are heard in the distance, hailing the occupants of the cottage. Amavi runs into the kitchen as soon as she sees them. There she hides and eavesdrops. The first man carries a long-necked gourd, with a chain of cowries around it; the second is holding a seedling; the third a fly whisk; and the fourth beads of cowries. Sewa comes out to give directions.

FIRST MAN: Where should I pour this?
SEWA: In this cup here. [*the man pours some red liquid into it. She takes it back into the room and returns*]
SECOND MAN: Where should I plant this? Where does he often pass water?
SEWA [*pointing to the bathroom*]: Plant it in the bathroom.
THIRD MAN [*throwing up the whisk and catching it*]: Now your husband is yours.

They steal away.

AMAVI [*coming out of hiding*]: I shall tell my husband about this.
SEWA [*scornfully*]: What?
AMAVI: That love potion of yours. You are a wicked girl. Is this the Agota type of city girl?

She runs into the bathroom, uproots the plant and throws it into the fire. She then pushes Sewa aside, brings out the cup and throws it far into the bush. Sewa looks on stolidly.

AMAVI: Eh! Is this what you women of Agota are? My husband will never use that cup. So you are turning my husband upside down? For the sole reason of loving you alone. That is why . . . I should think you have been trying your medicine on him already. He talks to himself and groans in the night. He is offended at the least remark of mine. The women of Agota! Your head is as hard as that of a tortoise. [*she stands and gazes at Sewa for some time*] If I bother about you I won't have time to do anything today. I must go to farm and get some food.

She picks up a big pan and leaves for the farm. As soon as she leaves, Kǫkutse re-enters.

SEWA [*rattling away before Kǫkutse can even step into the compound*]: Brother, Kǫkutse! Your wife is a wicked woman. She wants to kill you. [*pointing to the bathroom*] Go and look in the bathroom. [*Kǫkutse, without a word, runs into the bathroom*] Do you see the hole?

KǪKUTSE [*still in the bathroom*]: Yes, but what is it all about? [*becoming impatient*] Tell me. What is the matter?

SEWA: You know, whenever I go home my aunt asks me to warn you.

KǪKUTSE: Against what?

SEWA [*as if unwilling to mention the name*]: Kǫdzonǫ. She brought in some old women as soon as you left. They danced round her hearth, nasalizing a song. After that, Kǫdzonǫ, in front, they went to plant something in your bathroom. Then she brought out your cup, into which they poured a sort of black liquid. As soon as they had left, I threw the plant and the cup away.

KǪKUTSE: We shall see. Today! today! She will have to go home, even if it is night. Trying to kill me, so she can have my cacao all to herself and her children. I have anticipated her plans. Women! They think men are fools. Today we shall see.

Amavi re-enters under a heavy load of cassava.

AMAVI: Kǫdzotǫ, welcome.

Kǫkutse turns and slaps her in the face. She totters and falls with the load, the rim of the pan hitting Kǫkutse's right arm as he is about to slap her again. Meanwhile Sewa runs away.

KǪKUTSE: A stupid woman. A wicked woman. Pack your things and go to your father.

AMAVI [*rising on her knees and trembling*]: Ao! Is this what I deserve for all that I have done for you? Now that we are both jaded and tired from plodding all these years? You allow a foreign woman to turn your head against me. That witch of yours. Yes, I was here when her men came with their med . . .

KǪKUTSE: If you dare open your mouth again we shall see who is who. You think I have not found out all your wicked plots. It is your friendship with the women of Agota that has brought you into this. [*he raises a rubber sandal to slap her*]

AMAVI [*sobbing aloud*]: Yes, yes! Kill me. You have brought me here from Avegbe to kill in this wilderness. [*Kǫkutse gradually lowers his*

hand, trembling and breathing hard] Kill me for the witches of Agota to
feast upon. That is why I did not want to marry a farmer. I foresaw
all this, but my father forced me into it. It is my own fault. It is my
own fault.

KOKUTSE: Are you still there? Hey! Look! You witch, don't provoke me.
Don't tempt me. I say pack your things and go!

AMAVI [*face to the wall*]: I am not going anywhere. It is you who have
brought me here. I have not come to Agota of my own accord. You
must take me to my father.

KOKUTSE: Look! Do you think a crab's eye is wood? [*knocking his breast*]
I am a man; the master of my own house. From this very moment I
do not want to see you under my roof. [*scowling at her*] Trying to kill
me. What a fool. Despite our children. Hey! Sewa, bring all her
things out. Sewa! Are you, too, deaf. Don't you hear me!

*Kokutse goes after Sewa himself. Akọsua, a small girl of three years, comes out,
opening her arms to Amavi.*

AKỌSUA [*sobbing*]: Nana-na-na . . .

AMAVI [*looking upon her youngest daughter*]: Akọsua, don't weep, my
daughter. [*she picks her up and puts her on to her back. She shouts*] I have
come empty-handed; empty-handed I shall go. If God wills, I shall
eat. Akọsua, don't weep, do you hear? We shall soon reach home.
We shall soon see Tata once again.

Amavi exits. Musicians play.

SCENE NINE

*The scene is back in Avegbe Tonu at Agbeka's house. Agbeka, now an old man,
sits in his armchair, quaking his thighs. The chair is near the main door as usual,
and he has a small broom in hand for driving away flies. Pancra, a small boy of
five years, is playing beside him. The house looks deserted. Agbeka suddenly
stretches himself and exclaims loudly.*

PANCRA [*holding the chair*]: Papa, what is the matter?

AGBEKA [*rising to a sitting position*]: What is in my ear? Or, is a lorry
coming?

PANCRA [*running to the street and back*]: Papa, no lorry is coming.

AGBEKA [*shaking his head*]: I don't understand this. I have not been at
ease the whole day. Since Amavi's mother's death I have not been
myself. Look at the house, so deserted. I hope Kọkutse marries

another wife so that Amavi can come to stay with me. [*he dozes off, Pancra by his side. The musicians play softly.*]

Amavi enters the house unceremoniously. A child, completely wrapped up except for the head, is on her breast, its face hidden. She walks straight to Agbeka who stretches his hands, despite himself, to receive the child.

AGBEKA: Atoo! Tata's daughter. [*he is about to unwrap the cloth from her face, but Amavi holds his hand. Agbeka looks up into Amavi's face, confused for some time. Amavi also gazes into her father's face, speechless for some moments.*]

AMAVI: Akosua is dead. [*sobbing aloud, she kneels in front of her father*] See how you have treated me. You are the cause. You put me into the hands of death.

Some women and children begin flocking into the house.

AGBEKA [*tears trickling down his wrinkled face on hearing his daughter's words*] Pancra, go and call me the Odikro at once.

Pancra runs out.

FIRST WOMAN [*taking the child away*]: I will take the child for the meantime.

AGBEKA [*shaking his head and sighing*]: Amavi, be calm. We shall hear enough sobbing soon.

People come on to the stage and assemble around Amavi and her father. The town court officials arrive and a court is constituted. Amavi now sits on the ground in the centre, sobbing silently.

FIRST WOMAN: Ao! Amavi, what fate has brought you into this world. You too, your way is difficult!

LINGUIST: Silence please! Odikro welcomes our daughter.

SEVERAL VILLAGERS: Welcome, welcome . . .

LINGUIST [*addressing Agbeka*]: Togbui, Odikro puts it to you to ask your daughter 'amanie'.

AGBEKA [*biting his lips*]: Amavi, you are an old woman now, tell them. Tell them everything and let me hear too.

AMAVI [*blowing her nose into her cloth and composing herself*]: My husband drove me out of his hut.

AGBEKA [*uneasy at these words, cupping his hand to his right ear*]: Say that again and let them all hear. The people of Tonu, do you hear that?

LINGUIST: Togbui, be calm. We shall hear all. Amavi, tell us. How did it all happen.

AMAVI: Since I arrived at the cottage on the day I left here, Kodzoto had not been *giving me face*. He spent nights in town. Whenever I queried him, he took offence.

FIRST WOMAN: Those witches of Agota. I was saying . . .

LINGUIST: We have not come here for your comments, please!

AMAVI: One day he came from town with a girl following him. He called me to take my things to another room and make room for the girl, his new wife.

AGBEKA [*becoming more and more uneasy*]: My daughter to make room for a stranger.

AMAVI: Yesterday I saw four medicine men come into the house. The new wife, directing them, asked them to plant something in the bathroom. One poured some liquid into Kokutse's cup. Then the third man said: 'Now your husband is yours.' I understood those last words. So, as soon as they had left I uprooted the plant, throwing it into the fire. I took the cup and threw it far into the bush. Afterwards I left for the farm. Coming back with a load of cassava, I saw Kodzoto and said: 'Kodzoto, welcome.' At once he turned and slapped me in the face and I fell with the load. [*several are grumbling and Agbeka is squirming and beating his breast*] He called me a witch and ordered me out of his house. So I left the house, taking nothing except [*a pause*] Akosua and . . . this cloth . . . It was very dark when I was descending the slope. And since the path was stony and craggy I fell and rolled many times, with Akosua. When I got up after the last fall I could not see her face, but I felt her heart and she was still breathing.

FIRST WOMAN: Mothers, your lot is great.

AMAVI: When I came to the main road she cried feebly, and I gave her some water. Suddenly, she groaned, stretched herself, and at once she was cold. [*the people are greatly shocked*] I could not weep. I was simply confused. I had not a farthing on me. I could not pay for my own transport, let alone hire a lorry for a corpse. What could I do? Nothing! So I carried her on my back. Luckily, driver Amenyo's lorry was passing that morning. I told half my story; he agreed to bring me home free of charge. That is how I managed to arrive here.

LINGUIST: Did you tell the driver your child was dead?

AMAVI [*after a moment's silence*]: No, please.

SEVERAL VILLAGERS: Sorry, sorry. . . .

FIRST WOMAN: It pains, but what could you do?

AGBEKA [*eyes red, stamping his walking-stick on the floor, frantically pointing it at the people*]: All of you. You hear and see for yourselves. Today

Kọkutso, the son of Aflamato, has bathed my face in the sand. All this because I was unwise enough to give him my only daughter to marry. The people of Agota, tell me. . . . Is it because of money that Kọkutse should call my daughter a witch? It is a lesson! I have learnt it the hard way. . . . It is true. If you play too much with a dog it will lick your mouth. [*pauses bitterly*] Today's has passed already; tomorrow's will come!

SEVERAL VILLAGERS: Agbeka, be patient.

AN OLD MAN: How can you make a fool of your fellow man like that? And before a stranger too!

AGBEKA [*still shaking*]: It is simple; I gave you something. If it is no longer useful to you, why not give it back to me. Instead, you throw it away [*louder*] like a worn-out farm-shoe. Even then, you don't throw it away in the dark. Yet Kọkutse dare throw my only daughter into the darkness. And in a strange land too!

AKPLEZE, AN OLD MAN [*stretching out his hand*]: Amavitọ, stop, stop, altogether. It is piercing my ears. [*he stretches out to the Linguist as all eyes are on him*] Give me your staff. I, Akpleze, will bring Kọkutse to Avegbe Tonu, tonight.

ANOTHER OLD MAN: Yes, certainly, he must come to answer for this. This is too outrageous. He must not get away with this.

AGBEKA [*still musing, looking at his daughter and nodding his head*]: Amavi, you are right: I threw you away. Suppose something had happened to you in the dark? What on earth would Kọkutse have told me? All right! All is in the hands of God. [*drooping his head*] Amavinọ told me this. I am sorry she is no more. She is not here to hit this bald top of mine to stop me seeing Kọkutse's face any more. [*suddenly raising his head*] Look friends, go to your houses. I do not want any judgment in this matter. It serves me right.

All disperse as the Musicians play.

SCENE TEN

Some years have passed. Agbeka's house is gradually crumbling. Amavi sits alone on a small stool just inside her front door, looking very lonely. She covers herself with a faded, threadbare cloth, leaving only her face showing. She supports her chin with her two palms, resting her elbows on her thighs. She peers into the fire. A priest and a teacher pass by. The priest stops at the sight of Amavi. He keeps on looking at her very sadly. The teacher also looks into the priest's face.

TEACHER: That is a great woman.

PRIEST: Her look tells all.

TEACHER: Look how she cowers there. A devoted mother, more than any other that I have seen and heard of. Born untainted with sloth, she used to plod, drudge, for many years, I judge, with a cacao farmer in a selfless manner, hoping for a future.

PRIEST: Jilted, what future?

TEACHER: Mother dead, father dead, soon after, it is said. Sons still to learn to care for a mother, though there, alive and struggling hard, to climb life's ladder hard. This life is a chance game; her life demonstrates it.

A farmer in a smock joins them, wearing a skull-cap, a bag hanging at his side, and holding a cutlass.

FARMER [*also peering at Amavi enthralled, shaking his head*]: Ah! Brother, man is deep; world is wide, uncertain to decide. I am, also, a man. But there are men, not man. Kite picks not once, though one. When all is known that's done, many more are her sort to whose lot falls the . . . But to bear; she's unique! Endurance, where to seek love, hope . . . That is a great woman.

Rakinyo

'SEGUN AJIBADE

Rakinyo

CHARACTERS

AWERO, *Rakinyo's wife*

ELIZABETH, *Rakinyo's second wife*

RAKINYO

RAKINYO'S FATHER, *an old man*

ALHAJI, *Rakinyo's friend*

NEKAN, *another mutual friend*

BIMPE, *Rakinyo's third wife*

KANBI, *Rakinyo's uncle*

IBITOYE, *another uncle*

SIJU, *Rakinyo's aunt*

ODE, *a hunter*

THE POLICE SERGEANT

KOLA, *Bimpe's lawyer*

DEWALE, *a friend of Kola's*

The scene is set in a town in Western Nigeria.

It should be noted that this play has been written in blank verse. For reasons of space the speeches have been run on. However the capitals have been left in as an indication of line breaks for those who wish to use the blank verse rhythm. Others may find it more suitable to treat the speeches as conventional prose and they should ignore the capitals.

Publisher's Note

SCENE ONE

Rakinyo's room. Awero sits spinning when a knock is heard.

AWERO: Come in

Elizabeth enters.

> Oh Eli! How can you stay So far from me? Four days have passed
> Since I set my eyes on you last; Yet your route to the market Lies
> in front of our house.

ELIZABETH: If you hadn't seen me Couldn't you also trace me To find
out if something was wrong?

AWERO: Oh, you of all people Still talk like this! I expect you to
understand my plight More than anyone else. You know how it is
That we can't make ends meet. You know it. What time then have I
For rest or social contact? Even now when I should relax, See what
I am doing!

ELIZABETH: Awero, it is not that I am inconsiderate. It's my sympathy
for you that kept me away. I find it too pathetic to bear Whenever
I come to see you In this unbefitting state, I feel uneasy to stay on.

AWERO: This is a thing you need not mind Elizabeth. Our happy
friendship, after all, Started from our youth And fortune has kept us
together Even after each got married. No condition, therefore, of
either Should be so bad To keep us far apart.

ELIZABETH: My friend, I realize With deep understanding What you
are driving at, But the practice is too hard for me; I shed tears for
you in private Any time I visit you here. I truly feel something
pricking my heart.

AWERO: Elizabeth, let me frankly tell you today; I always want you here.
Your presence drives away my depression And erases my gloom;
Your chatting puts in me, a new life To cope with my difficulties
With greater courage.

ELIZABETH: But, friend, one fault of yours, The greatest that you have,
Is obstinacy. How many times haven't I suggested, Out of my great
love for you, How you can earn a better living? But, as if this man
is your god, Or, as if he has charmed you, You say you will die with
him.

AWERO: As for leaving the man, I would find it difficult. He has not
offended me in any way. Although he is poor, he loves me well.
We have health and peace of mind And that is all that matters in
life.

ELIZABETH: Do you say you have peace of mind When you are being drowned In the foaming sea of poverty? What peace of mind do you have When you haven't got gold ear-rings, Trinkets, fashionable shoes, Gorgeous and up-to-date dresses, And all that make you a real woman?

AWERO: Ha!

ELIZABETH: Look at the many wives of Alhaji, Your husband's friend. They are all well provided for; And this constitutes their happiness And peace of mind. Consider Mrs Awe, Mrs Smith, And all the rest in their circle. Can you stand them? If all women are out For a prestige social gathering, Can you appear among them? Sit down in this veritable den, And claim peace of mind. You are being ruined by imagination, Let me tell you.

AWERO: Ha!

ELIZABETH: Why, it is natural with women And we can't be blamed for it. If you want who is culpable, It is nature. God has created us with that urge – Love and appreciation of beauty. Are you then not a woman any more?

AWERO: I am a woman but . . .

ELIZABETH: But what, Awero? Even the health you claim is no health. It is a pity you have no mirror here, But if you don't mind, I shall take you to my room Where you can stand naked In front of my dressing mirror And see things for yourself. You are wasting away fast! The hollows of your shoulders Can each hold a bottle of water; Your beauty which was unparalleled Before you entered into this hell Has faded away completely, And you are as beautiful as no one again! These are the results of bad living.

AWERO: Can this be true?

ELIZABETH: It is true, girl! Good living, that is the thing That can keep you healthy; And your life-span will be short without it.

AWERO: Then I think we have to work harder To improve our living standards.

ELIZABETH: Are you still talking of working harder When you are already bent Under the yoke of hard labour? Do something about yourself And be quick with it. Our lives are so short these days That we have no time to waste. By the way, How much does he give For your daily chop-money?

AWERO: The least ever given is four shillings, But he occasionally hits seven.

ELIZABETH: Yes, and what more?

AWERO: Nothing more. That is all he is able to give.

ELIZABETH: W-h-a-t! Is this all you live upon? And you take pride in this? I marvel at you! Look, as I go to the market now, My man gave me one pound. [*produces money*]

AWERO: One pound at a blow!

ELIZABETH: But is this anything? I refused it at first But had to accept it After a long persuasion. He knows I won't have anything to do With this type of scanty sum.

AWERO: Do you say one pound at a blow is scanty?

ELIZABETH: And so, one pound for a whole morning Is something to you again? Anyway, you have converted yourself To a beast of burden here. Sit down there. You will die one day And there will be no money To buy ordinary calico for your corpse! Which reminds me, Does he buy you clothes at all – A man who can't afford four shillings For the market?

AWERO: To speak my mind, he buys me clothes But they are inferior types. Anyway, the lace he bought recently Is of a good quality.

ELIZABETH: Let me see it then.

AWERO: Right, I am coming.

Awero exits.

ELIZABETH: This damned fool needs to learn a lesson. An ungrateful woman Who is given four to seven shillings And doesn't appreciate it! She is bought cloths regularly But complains of poverty more loudly every day. She has not seen life! She doesn't know that All of us beam with smiles outside Only to cover up the sorrows at home. If she has realized that we all hire The gorgeous dresses and ornaments We put on on occasions, She should have learnt To sing Rakinyo's praise daily. My husband has nothing to give me; I feed him instead. If I get a husband like Awero's, Shouldn't I thank my stars?

Awero returns, unwrapping the cloth.

Why have you delayed so much?

AWERO: Oh, sorry, I misplaced the key Of my box.

ELIZABETH: There seems to be no order In your house here. The box key also Hasn't got a place of its own! All right, let me see the cloth.

[*Awero uncovers the cloth*]

AWERO: Here it is.

ELIZABETH: W-h-a-t! Is this your superior quality material? This is exactly the type My house-girl refused to wear To the market last

week. I bought it, thinking it was good For a servant of her type;
But she refused it bluntly. She however agreed to wear it in the
kitchen.

AWERO: An ordinary servant refusing this! Then life is easy there.

ELIZABETH: You can continue To take pride in hardship. I have no
more time for you – Off to the market.

AWERO: Wait, first, Elizabeth. But – but do you think that If I leave this
man now I will get a man of good standing To marry me?

ELIZABETH: Come, your beauty is only hiding Somewhere within you.
Take a month's complete rest Under your father's roof And eat
good food. You'll see the beauty reappearing. That will be a charm
to men Who will rush at you As fishes do to baits. You can then
pick and choose.

AWERO: So?

ELIZABETH: That is all the truth about you.

AWERO: You will hear of me soon.

ELIZABETH: You may not be long To hear of me also. For I may, in a
few days, Be in another man's house.

AWERO: Another man's house! Why would you choose to leave A man
who cares for you so much?

ELIZABETH: Do you call that good care? I consider it a life of hardship;
And I have to look for a better life. After all, men are always
proposing. Why shouldn't I consider one of them, If I am assured
of a happier life?

AWERO: Men do propose to you indeed; But why do they ignore me?

ELIZABETH: Much depends on how you make yourself. You are not
sociable – always on the farm Or spinning in the room. How can
men notice your existence? Even if a few happen to meet you They
will cast a glance at you And go their way unaffected. The beauty
to shake their hearts Has vanished in you!

AWERO: Oh Lord save me! The charming beauty truly has vanished;
Or else why should men see me and go Without their hearts
jumping within their chest? I must do something about myself this
time.

ELIZABETH: Well, I am off to the market. I may call on you on my
return If I don't have a lift.

Elizabeth goes out.

AWERO: 'If I don't have a lift'! It is true. She is sociable. All men know
her and would not hesitate To pick her up in their cars. See me
here. Who knows me? Who would ever give me a lift? Instead, they

will sweep me off the road With their long cars. Now I see that I need a change. I have been blind for too long a time And have been living in the past. I shall now move with time And enter into a circle befitting me. She says my shoulder hollows are deep And I can feel them even now. Well, it's the result of worries and overwork. Fortunately, Elizabeth says my beauty is only hidden. I shall go to relax and regain it. Then I shall go into another man's house Where I shall sleep soundly on a golden bed And open my eyes only to hear a gentle knock By a servant calling me to tea! I shall go . . .! To ride in 220 super And wave to every acquaintance we meet Is a pleasant thing. Occasionally, I shall stop my husband For some short conversation With close acquaintances and friends . . . Perhaps Elizabeth herself. I'll always be in high heels and gorgeous dresses And make sure no woman beats me At parties or when we go shopping. No, my attitude must change from now! Rakinyo – will return to find me different.

She pushes her work aside. Rakinyo enters, and soon notices her manner.

RAKINYO: Missis, why are you in this mood? [*no reply*] Is there anything wrong? [*no reply*] Are you ill? [*no reply*]

Rakinyo touches her forehead but has his hand knocked away.

What is wrong? Why do you behave like this, missis? Don't be a child. I will go for drug now, Or we consult Doctor Coker. He is always ready to help us.

AWERO: Look, leave me alone And don't disturb my peace of mind. There is no time you return And don't have obnoxious questions to ask.

RAKINYO: What is obnoxious about my attempt To remove the cause of your sorrowful look? I don't think that I have ever had the occasion To ask you this sort of question. And yet you say I disturb you always. You know how very little I poke my nose into women's affairs . . .

AWERO: Will you leave me to myself And go your own way!

RAKINYO: Go my own way? Am I not the right person To know your troubles?

AWERO: You are the wrong person. You talk like a person Who has the solution to my problems.

RAKINYO: Am I not your husband?

AWERO: Ha, ha, ha, you make me laugh! If all men claim to be husbands, Do you also claim to be one?

RAKINYO: Yes, and a good one too!

AWERO: Do you call yourself a good husband? You don't merit it.

RAKINYO: I merit it.

AWERO: In which ways?

RAKINYO: If nothing at all, I have kept you In my house For five good years. We don't borrow Neither do we steal.

AWERO: Why don't you go borrowing? I bet I wouldn't have spent The first night with you.

RAKINYO: I never go borrowing Because such is not the practice In our family. I am poor though, Yet I have maintained you To this day Without borrowing, or stealing.

AWERO: Tweaa! My maintainer! Nonsense! What have you done for me Since I entered your house? Old-fashioned dresses . . . The type servants reject In other houses.

RAKINYO: I am surprised at you. Your behaviour is unusual today.

AWERO: My eyes are now opened. I am no longer ready To live in the past.

RAKINYO: What do you mean by that? We move with time And live up-to-date enough.

AWERO: Claiming undue glory As you are doing now Is a sign of men afflicted With inherited poverty.

RAKINYO: Inherited poverty! From where?

AWERO: From your ancestors: As far back as people can remember, Your great-grandfather was a pauper. Your grandmother died of overwork To which she was forced By her husband's poverty. And as for your father, We of the present day know How great his poverty is. They have handed this poverty down to you. And you want to transfer it to me And to my children. But . . .

RAKINYO: How can you insult my family? So mercilessly!

AWERO: What else can one do With a generation of hopeless paupers?

RAKINYO: Nonsense! If you don't take time, I will make you swallow All that you vomited just now. [*he moves towards her as if to hit her*]

AWERO: What can you do? Son of the sons of paupers!

RAKINYO: I can slap you [*he slaps her, and then begins to beat her. Awero tries to offer resistance at first; finding it useless, she tries to escape, but Rakinyo prevents her. She cries for help*]

AWERO: I'm dead oh! He's killed me, oh! Neighbours help, help! He's killed me, oh . . .

Rakinyo's father, an old man enters.

OLD MAN: Rakinyo, Rakinyo, [*holding him*] Why do you beat your wife As if she is not a human being? Throughout your five years' stay together, I never had cause To intervene like this before. What is the cause of this big fight?

RAKINYO: When I returned home And found her sad, I asked for the cause. Her reply was a rain of insults On me and my family. Verbal persuasion would not make her stop; She annoyed me more and more, And so I tried the hand And now she is shouting.

AWERO: Papa, don't mind him. You vex oh, you no vex oh; I shall leave your house today. My pin is the smallest; I won't leave it behind.

OLD MAN: You don't settle quarrels By annoying and getting annoyed. You, Rakinyo, are wrong To have beaten your wife. I am at home – in the next room. Why can't you report her to me? At worst you could by-pass me To report her to her father. He could scold or even beat her If she is found guilty. You must never give her such a beating again.

AWERO: Old man, I say leave him. I will go to another man And you will soon see me in saloon cars. You will not be able to look In my direction twice.

RAKINYO: Now, I see the cause of your change. Some men are promising you heaven. Go to them without delay; I shall also meet my luck somewhere else. No hen is ever so unlucky As to lay black eggs.

OLD MAN: No, no, no, you people should be reasonable! This is not how lovers Should go about their misunderstandings. You must desist from making statements That could drive you apart. This quarrel is a small thing Which can be settled amicably.

AWERO: What kind of small thing, old man, Do you call this quarrel? He has laid his hands on me already. The egg that is smashed Cannot be made whole again, He has brought a speedy end To my stay in his house, Right now, I am going to pack.

OLD MAN: No, don't do that . . .

RAKINYO: Leave her, my father. Let her go. You are at liberty to pack But not what I bought With my own money.

AWERO: I have the full right To pack all that you bought for me. Didn't I bear children for you? Your articles are the reward For my labour over your children.

RAKINYO: O.K., clear off from my presence. And make sure you spend not more Than ten minutes For your packing.

AWERO: Ten minutes! Too much. Check up after five And you will find me gone!

She goes out.

OLD MAN: Awero, Awero, come back . . .! Come back I say! . . .
[*there is no reply*] Rakinyo, go and bring her back.

RAKINYO: My father, I have told you Let her go.

OLD MAN: Is this how your marriage will end?

RAKINYO: Father, that is it. She is dreaming of a better man. She will
suffer in this town And how I will laugh at her . . . No small!

OLD MAN: The head of a baby On its mother's back Should not tilt
Where there are elders. I must go and meet her parents.

RAKINYO: Father, don't move a step Towards Awero's father's house.
When I married her, Did I introduce her father to you? And did I
introduce you to her parents? Who then will you say you are If you
reach her father's house? You saw us married, And you have seen
us part. That is all, father; Rest your soul.

OLD MAN: The world has spoilt, Our society has been badly affected
By customs we acquire from nowhere . . . Strange customs that have
no meaning. In our own time . . . the good old days . . . Your parents
married for you, And you couldn't divorce Because you didn't choose
The one you were marrying. But what operates today? Our children
expect a first baby Or even a second Before informing their parents
That they are married! But when you talk They say you are old,
You don't know what constitutes happiness. Your wives are picked
by the roadside And, like a child's disgusting plaything, You cast them
away. Is this sadness or happiness? You of today will break the
world Into minute fragments. But before then, Let us go first.

*He goes off and Rakinyo sits down, disconcerted. There is a pause – the lights are
dimmed or music is played – to indicate a brief passage of time, then Alhaji,
Nekan and Elizabeth enter.*

ALHAJI: Rakinyo, keep heart. Your case has become The talk of the
town, And that is why we rush down To know the true cause.

RAKINYO: I returned from the farm To find her sad And, asking to
know the cause, She flared up And rained insults on me And on my
ancestors.

NEKAN: What manner of behaviour was that?

RAKINYO: It was clearer than spring water That she wanted a divorce.
Not finding any pretext, She resorted to that trick. I can tolerate
much of a woman's insult But not that on my ancestors.

ALHAJI: And so she left?

RAKINYO: And so I gave her a beating. My father was however right

there To stop me from beating her much. He threw in soothing words
Which fell on Awero's deaf ear. She packed and left, Leaving my
father in embarrassment.

ELIZABETH: She wouldn't even give the grey hair Some respect!

RAKINYO: Ah, that is the strange character Your friend developed
In the space of a forenoon.

ALHAJI: Nekan, our annoyance Is no more necessary. If the grey hair
also falls a prey To Awero's malicious design, What chance do we
babies stand?

NEKAN: But we must implement our plan.

ALHAJI: As Allah exists, That must come to pass. Rakinyo, could you
believe, Soon as we heard the news, We met her at her father's
house, Thinking that she would respect us.

NEKAN: If you witnessed the sort of insults Awero passed on us today . . .
They are better not recounted. They could make a man weep
publicly.

ALHAJI: We did not weep; And we shall not weep. But the disgrace
Awero brought on us today, She will have ten-fold from us.

NEKAN: Not to mince words, Our arrangements are completed To see
another wife in your house As soon as possible.

ALHAJI: In the meantime, Elizabeth, Awero's friend, Will take care of
you.

RAKINYO: But how can she leave her husband To come and take care of
me?

ELIZABETH: That marriage is broken please.

RAKINYO: Since when did this happen?

ELIZABETH: Not quite a week ago.

RAKINYO: But you never mentioned it.

ELIZABETH: Yes, because I do not want to wash My stained cloth in
public And open myself up to ridicule.

RAKINYO: What happened?

ELIZABETH: I discovered over two months ago That my man was a
husband To more than five other women in town. I objected on the
grounds that He was always impoverished By too many women's
bills, But this was to no avail. When, ultimately, I refused To cook
for him with my own money, He sacked me, And I left without
question.

RAKINYO [*doubtfully*]: My friends, do you say yes To these things?

NEKAN: Our answer is yes. Trust, we cannot bring trouble upon you.
This conclusion has been reached After careful thought and
investigation.

RAKINYO: In any case, Since you propose That I shouldn't be long
In getting married, I think I can spare Elizabeth All the troubles.

NEKAN: The emphasis, my friend, is not On getting you another wife as
such. It is on getting you the type of woman Who will be a direct
answer To the challenge thrown by Awero.

RAKINYO: But, Elizabeth, didn't you tell me Sometime ago That you
had a friend Who was dead in love with me? What about that
person?

ELIZABETH: I have no friend with whom I share such secrets. I was
only trying to pull your leg.

RAKINYO: Alhaji, don't you feel that Since Elizabeth's fate is also in the
balance She will need sometime to herself To re-plan her affairs?
I think I can manage things alone Till I get married.

ALHAJI: Rakinyo, let this woman take care of you. It's part of our
design To teach Awero a lesson. To refuse this offer now Is to double
or even triple our disgrace Which is already almost unbearable. I am
sure, you will not be long To change your mind about her. She is a
good woman, I assure you.

RAKINYO: I shall not refuse her As she is also willing to help me.

ELIZABETH: Oh, I am prepared to help you Through the difficult time.

ALHAJI: Whatever it will cost To make you live happily, Rakinyo, We
are there.

NEKAN: Rakinyo, never fear. As we go now, We shall make Awero and
her relatives Who are firmly behind her Understand that you have
not been shamed.

ALHAJI: We shall make them know That if any of the thousands of stars
That litter the heaven Disappears now, Another will take its place
immediately. We shall leave now But we shall return soon To set
you on the path to a better life.

NEKAN: As for Elizabeth, We shall still have A heart to heart talk with
you Concerning her. We shall return soon.

RAKINYO: Thank you my friends.

Nekan and Alhaji go out.

Elizabeth, I am sorry I have to bother you With my own problems
At a time you need peace of mind most.

ELIZABETH: Never mind, Rakinyo. I have chosen to make this sacrifice
Only to save you from disgrace.

RAKINYO: I am very grateful, Elizabeth For this big sacrifice on your
part.

ELIZABETH: What is actually the matter With Awero?

RAKINYO: She says I don't provide For her enough.

ELIZABETH: Look, she is shallow minded! Which man has enough To satisfy women today? She doesn't know that We smile and talk big Only to comfort ourselves. You work hard and provide For Awero and her children, Yet she cries louder each day Of insufficiency and poverty As if we who are silent Have money spring in our rooms.

RAKINYO: I tried my best, But in sincerity, I hardly gave More than four shillings.

ELIZABETH: Did Gbonka* ever do more Than trying his best To become our hero? You did well to give four shillings. I had to feed my husband! Will you not be ashamed For your wife to feed you all along Without your effort to contribute?

RAKINYO: In fact, I will be ashamed.

Awero enters in rage, girding her loins firmly with her head-tie and dragging her second piece of cloth behind her.

AWERO [*to Elizabeth*]: You serpent! Viper! Adder! Devil! Is this the trick you are up to? You receive ten pounds every morning, What do you want here now?

She attempts to slap Elizabeth who is also ready for a fight but Rakinyo grabs Awero's hand before it can land.

RAKINYO: What are you about to do? Do you think your departure is my end? You think I have no sympathizers? This is a sweet vengeance on you.

AWERO: I have not come to you, Rakinyo. So leave me. It is this rogue I want. She is a real devil . . .

RAKINYO: What right have you to insult her? If you are still here in the next minute, I will squeeze life out of you!

He lets go of her hand. Alhaji and Nekan enter.

ALHAJI: Awero, what things of your's Still remain here? It is only a shameless person Who returns to a place Where she has already bade good night.

AWERO: I have not returned here, And I shall not. I have only come to To give your new wife A piece of kolanut to chew.

NEKAN: You have lost that right now. You have no more say in this house. Get back to your father's house And be their queen. Is that not what you want?

AWERO: I do not blame you For your wrong stand in this case. It's only

---

*Gbonka – a hero in Yoruba history.

she and I who know Why I have the right To jump on her And lash her with my tongue.

RAKINYO: What right have you? You decided to shame me And she saved my face. So you thought you were my end? Come, let me tell you; Just as fishes are in thousands In the sea, And stars are in millions In the sky, So also are women uncountable In the world, And sympathizers are endless On earth. Let one go this moment And another will replace her in the next.

AWERO: The secret is that . . .

Alhaji and Nekan rush up on Awero.

ALHAJI: Awero, off, off now! If not, we'll call the police in.

AWERO: Before your police come, I will have gone.

RAKINYO: Gentlemen, don't you worry. She obeys nothing but beating. I will give her that And you will see how obedient She can be.

Rakinyo goes out to get a whip.

AWERO: Elizabeth, I have a last message for you. The broom with which you sweep me Out of this house, The same broom will be used In sweeping you out also. Yee . . . yee . . . yee . . .

Awero runs out, crying with rage.

RAKINYO: May Sango* strike you dead. Rat!

NEKAN: Rakinyo, leave that thief alone And come to listen to us.

Rakinyo returns with whip.

Alhaji, go to the business; We have little time to spend.

ALHAJI: We've heard of a highly yielding trade And we have borrowed this money For you to start with. You will carry palm oil to the north And bring back groundnut oil, Cotton thread, hides and skin Which are in great demand here. Try it and let us see How it works. There is another highly risky But highly yielding secret trade . . .

ELIZABETH: Excuse me, gentlemen. It seems the rest of the discussion Is meant for the man's ear. You will therefore allow me To move to the kitchen.

NEKAN: Thank you, good woman. You are allowed.

Elizabeth exits.

This woman has etiquette, Doesn't she?

---

*Sango – god of thunder.

ALHAJI: That's a question for Rakinyo to answer, Not for me.

RAKINYO: Oh well, she has.

NEKAN: If you agree she has etiquette, Then start to think seriously About her. [*They all laugh.*]

ALHAJI: The secret trade is highly yielding, Depending on your courage and luck. It involves putting all your fortune into it. If fortune accompanies you, You can become the richest In the province overnight. If luck shuns your company, You can become the man With the greatest debt to pay. This is where the need for courage lies – The courage to risk all – Fortune and life itself! You will run, jump, dodge And play dead; All to avoid falling into their hands, Over to you. Choose which one you like.

RAKINYO: Whoever wants to make a great gain Must be prepared for a heavy loss. He who cannot take risks Cannot also do business. I shall put in all I have. If it turns against me, I don't care; I am used to poverty. If I lose my life in the venture, This is my farewell to you.

NEKAN: The amount we could raise Is not sufficient for the trade. Expand it first by starting With this north to south trade. No waste of time. You are starting tomorrow. Alhaji, give the arrangement to him And let us go.

ALHAJI: Well, here is five hundred pounds.

RAKINYO: Thank you my friends!

NEKAN: Count them. [*Rakinyo wants to start counting immediately*]

ALHAJI: Not now. We shall go To bring you some handkerchiefs. The world we live in is a difficult one – More difficult than you can imagine!

NEKAN: We shall not leave you alone. As long as we live, Your parrot will never perish Where it goes to fetch its daily food. When the hand takes food to the mouth, It returns safely. So shall your going and coming Be perfectly safe.

RAKINYO: Ase.

NEKAN: Go and get ready.

RAKINYO: Thank you oh!

NEKAN: There is no need Thanking oneself.

Rakinyo is about to leave.

ALHAJI: Wait, Rakinyo. There is no better time To discuss this matter with you. I don't think this woman, Elizabeth, Is bad for you.

RAKINYO [*surprised*]: Alhaji!

ALHAJI: Take it easy, man. This is only a suggestion. After you have studied her And you are satisfied that She is good enough for you,

Then you can make up your mind About her. But I advise you,
Consider her seriously.

RAKINYO: Alhaji, this is A little bit unexpected.

NEKAN: No. Rakinyo, We have only proposed it to you And you can
turn it over In your mind And take your decision. We are going.

RAKINYO [*sighs*]: All right. Thank you. I will think of it And let you
hear My decision.

ALHAJI: Right, bye for now.

Nekan and Alhaji exit.

RAKINYO [*bewildered*]: So my friends' design Is to make me marry this
woman . . . She is my wife's friend . . . [*pause*] I don't think I can
marry her. If I do now, What will the world Think about me? Yet,
how do I let my friends down? I cannot offend them! But, oh, the
public opinion . . .! What will the world think of me If I should
marry my wife's friend? [*pause*] Right, I think I am not being
realistic! Did Awero think of public opinion When divorcing me
disgracefully? Why then should I bother About the public opinion?
I shall have Elizabeth And that will serve Awero right.

SCENE TWO

Rakinyo has made a fortune. His room is richly furnished. He enters.

RAKINYO: I will kill; I will capture; These are the two ambitions With
which man goes to war. I went to my own war, Prepared to kill and
to capture; And also to be killed or be captured. But God was
behind me; I killed and captured – And captured in large quantities.
Who would ever say, a short while ago, That Rakinyo would be a
money man? Who would dare to predict, before my divorce, That
Rakinyo would build mansions And buy long cars for pleasure?
This is fortune for which I thank my star. My star, let me have
cause to thank you And thank you more and more Till the end of
my journey.

Elizabeth, his wife, enters sorrowfully.

Why do you look so sad, Elizabeth? Are you ill?

ELIZABETH: Husband, let me unfold to you The secret chambers of my
mind. I have not been happy since you opened The cloth that
covers the matter Between you and that girl.

RAKINYO: Why should this affect you so much? It is no secret. I want her for my second wife, And I don't think it is wrong To let you smell something of it Before she comes.

ELIZABETH: It is the idea of her coming, And nothing more, That injures me, husband.

RAKINYO: Elizabeth, look here; You don't mean to prevent me From marrying a second wife. I didn't enter into such a bargain with you.

ELIZABETH: Husband, don't misunderstand me. You have a right to marry As many as will satisfy you; It is that girl I detest. I know what she could be; I can't cope with her. Besides, she's not a good choice For a lucky person like you.

RAKINYO: I wonder why you women Lose four of your five senses Any time your interests are affected. Don't you see that I have the cash To control her with And that that is all that matters? I shall tame her And make her behave The way I like.

ELIZABETH: How can an ant succeed Where elephants have failed? Is it ever possible to tame a leopard To the extent of eating grass? Husband, think twice Before you embark Upon this venture.

RAKINYO: Mind you, you are only a woman. My desires should be satisfied And my words shall be final. Bimpe is to be married; That is all.

ELIZABETH: The day Bimpe enters your house, That same day I shall go!

RAKINYO: The earlier you go, the better. A woman can't make herself The husband in my house here.

ELIZABETH: Good, I can hear your friends' voices. They are coming here. I shall put the matter before them again And see what they have to say.

Alhaji and Nekan enter.

RAKINYO: You are welcome, friends; You couldn't have come better. Here is a woman Trying to make herself a man.

NEKAN: How?

RAKINYO: She wants to claim the right To choose for me, Who to marry And who not to marry.

ALHAJI: It is this same case Which she mentioned to us That has brought us here. Do you still desire to marry the girl?

RAKINYO: The arrangements are completed; Fixing the date is in my hand. I think I mentioned this to you yesterday.

ALHAJI: And you don't want to listen To your wife's advice?

RAKINYO: I don't want to. I can't see a woman's view prevailing In a house where there is a man.

NEKAN: Rakinyo, don't you know that When the owl cries at noon
And the wild antelope breaks into the market In broad daylight,
There must be a cause? Don't you know that When the ape chases
the dog away, And a human passes The faeces of a goat, There
must be a reason? It is this cause, my friend, That you should look
for Instead of holding so firm, Without due consideration, To an
age-long tradition!

RAKINYO: Nekan, Alhaji, my friendship with you Is not a day old.
It started from our youth. Which of you can stomach it When a
woman attempts to take The control of the house from him? Which
of you will yield to a woman's advice When he is already decided
Upon a course of action? Let such a person come out boldly To
advise me to subject myself To a woman's device.

ALHAJI: Nekan, admonition has developed A deadly boil in its mouth.
How then can it speak? Truly, I can't tolerate a woman Trying to
dictate to me in any form. I had thought this to be a special case
Needing some form of consideration But the way in which our
friend Has put the whole case now Gums our lips together.

NEKAN: Alhaji, this is nothing. It is not always that advice is acceptable.
Therefore we should drop this matter. This does not rule out the
fact That we can amicably advise him On other matters. So,
Rakinyo, we wish you luck And wish you take a stand That is most
beneficial to you. That will be to our happiness. Alhaji, what do you
say to that?

ALHAJI: That is all.

NEKAN: Well, we shouldn't be too long In going to the garage To
finalize the arrangement About the transportation of cotton prints
To the north.

ALHAJI: Thank you Nekan; I've almost forgotten. Rakinyo, we are
leaving you now; Time is against us. I hope you will let us know
Your decision by and by.

RAKINYO: I shall be in your house To tell you.

ELIZABETH: Alhaji, please don't go yet – two of you. I want to put a
question to Rakinyo In your presence So that you serve as my
witnesses.

Bimpe enters.

Ehch, here comes the devil That fishes in others' pools! Bimpe,
there is no place for you In this house. Rakinyo cannot be your
husband. Turn back right now And return to where you came from.

BIMPE: Why don't you give your soul a rest, mama? Nature has not

created The world of Rakinyo For you alone. We shall all taste of
it.

ELIZABETH: You shall not taste of it! If his life is created For every other
woman, It is definitely not for you.

BIMPE: What! Do I walk on four legs; Or am I turned inside out?
What you successfully did somewhere, You can't repeat it here.
Not to me!

ELIZABETH: I shall see to it That it is made clear to you That your
seat is not in Rakinyo's house.

BIMPE: So long as your husband will have me, My seat is as firm as
yours.

ELIZABETH: Husband, will you have this girl?

RAKINYO: I will, and will have you also.

ELIZABETH: You won't have me together with this girl. Alhaji, I shall
leave this house with you. But remember, Rakinyo, There is going
to be a time When you will put your finger Into your eyes And
tears will not flow.

RAKINYO: When the heart is decided, No amount of threat can change
it. But bear in mind, The step you are taking now Has no hand of
mine in it.

ELIZABETH: Alhaji, thank you for all your troubles. Mr Nekan, I thank
you also For all you have done. I shall enter to pack and leave. I shall
see the two of you later.

Elizabeth exits.
Alhaji and Nekan exchange looks of surprise.

RAKINYO: Friends, my stand is clear in this case. I've only told her not
to decide for me; But she cannot have a husband Who is not to be
decided for; And so she left. I have not offended her in any way.

NEKAN: Rakinyo . . . you know . . . but . . . I . . .

BIMPE: Good gentlemen, You don't have to be so much surprised At this
development of events. It is the fear of Elizabeth's shadow That
sacks her and nothing else. She ousted a woman From her husband's
house And she knows that I have an inner knowledge Of her
clandestine activities. I have come here To live with her in peace
and harmony And not to oust her. Yet she decided to leave. How,
gentlemen, do you understand This course of action?

NEKAN: Elizabeth you mean?

BIMPE: That is her work. Those who know her Will give no different
testimony. She is so clever with it That she wins everybody to her
side. She is a real devil.

ALHAJI: Elizabeth ousted a woman From her husband's house?
BIMPE: With the devil's cleverness, She outwitted her!

Alhaji and Nekan exchange looks of confusion.

ALHAJI: When cases become muddled, And confusion mounts confusion,
The wise himself becomes stupified, And talks nothing but madness.
Therefore come, my friend. Let us leave Rakinyo to his discretion
And wish him the best As we see to our own business.
NEKAN: Rakinyo, we shall leave. We hope to see you some time.
RAKINYO: Bimpe, I will see them off. Make yourself at home.
BIMPE: Right, my good gentlemen, I wish you luck as well.
ALL: Goodbye.

Rakinyo, Alhaji and Bimpe exit.

BIMPE: The head that will wear the golden crown Will never miss it.
Either his luck like wind Blows the crown towards him, Or his star
like river current Carries him to the crown. The greatest obstacle is
out of my way; I have come face to face With Rakinyo's big money.
I must make full use of any chances That may come my way; For
men are inconsistent in their love. As he is glad to sack Elizabeth for
me today, So also may he be glad one day, To rid himself of me for
another woman. My star and my luck, Blow good towards me!

SCENE THREE

*Rakinyo's dining-table is half prepared. He enters rather hurriedly and looks round
for somebody.*

RAKINYO: Who's there? Bimpe!
BIMPE: My husband!

Bimpe rushes in.

RAKINYO: Is the food ready?
BIMPE: It's about ready.
RAKINYO: They will be here within the next few minutes.
BIMPE: You never told me – Are they coming with their wives?
RAKINYO: Wives! Nekan alone has enough wives To fill every space
here; And Alhaji has more!
BIMPE: Well, they may choose To bring one wife each.

RAKINYO: No man, not wanting to cause trouble, Takes one of many
    wives out On an occasion such as this.

BIMPE: Then we are only four.

RAKINYO: Four and that is all. Quick. See that the food is here in time.
    Alhaji doesn't like delays.

Bimpe exits. Alhaji and Nekan enter.

    Oh, you are welcome, gentlemen. Bimpe had been so much concerned
    About your food getting cold. She has however decided To keep it
    on fire Till I had informed her you were in.

NEKAN: Then you have got a good wife. I like women who are alive to
    their duties. If my eldest wife had been half as good, I wouldn't
    have married two.

ALHAJI: And if any of my wives Had been quarter as good, She could
    have won me to herself alone.

RAKINYO: Thank you for these compliments. Have your seats while I
    dash To inform her you are in.

Rakinyo exits.

NEKAN: If this woman truly behaves like this, She is good. But she is too
    costly. I learnt every relative of Bimpe Has had houses built or
    bought for him By Rakinyo.

ALHAJI: The irony of it all is that No relative of Rakinyo Has ever owed
    him a tent! And how do you advise him against this? How do you
    make Rakinyo realize That women are birds that fly away Soon as
    the tree branch breaks? We must be spectators Till time permits us to
    come in.

Rakinyo enters, followed by Bimpe carrying food.

RAKINYO: Well gentlemen, We can now join your company And fill full.
    Let us cut this for appetite. [*they drink wine while Bimpe serves the food*]
    Friends, over to you. There should be no ceremony; No waste of time.
    The food musn't be allowed to get cold. Therefore, share our love.
    [*they eat*]

BIMPE: May I seize this opportunity, husband, To ask if you would mind
    Building a house for my mother At Ehindi?

RAKINYO: I guess she was one of the first To have houses bought for them.

BIMPE: Oh yes, that is true, dear, But you know, we did it in a hurry
    And we couldn't buy a fashionable one. Besides, since we don't
    remit to her regularly, She needs a source of income Befitting my
    mother. As for my father, for example, I wouldn't expect you to do

much more. Men can always get on with little, But definitely not
women.

RAKINYO: Bimpe, I think what we have done Should be sufficient for
her. If we hadn't been rich, She wouldn't have got Even what you
say is not fashionable.

BIMPE: Right, Rakinyo, I'm sure you still remember The case of my
senior brother You and I discussed. You know, the road to his office
Which is so bad and rough That the Morris Minor we gave him
Is, as you can see, worn out now. I suppose we could get him – a
Benz Or, say, a Peugeot Which can both stand such rough roads.

RAKINYO: Bimpe, let us try to think About ourselves also And not only
of your relatives All the time. It is sea which never dries up; Not
money. If we do not learn to take care of money As a visitor is cared
for, It will desert us. And what a disgrace it is To come from riding
on horseback To walking on foot! So, please, slow down a bit. The
plantain bears fruit but once.

BIMPE: In that case, I will ask for one last favour.

RAKINYO: What favour again, Bimpe?

BIMPE: My brother's salary, you know, Is not sufficient to maintain a car.

RAKINYO: Yes I know that.

BIMPE: So, if we could supply him with fuel . . .

RAKINYO: But, Bimpe, don't we give him A regular remittance for this
cause?

BIMPE: Oh yes, husband, I know this. But you must try to understand
me And my problems with me. I mean, this is just a further help.
My brother, after all, is your brother. Look, husband, if this is done,
It will add a star to your crown In the eyes of my relatives. One
does not have to count the cost If a big name is to be gained.

RAKINYO: Bimpe, I think I must tell you Point blank, right now, that
I am fed up with your demands. I have done more than enough
For your people and yet Every day sees you making Fresh demands.
How much have you seen me do For my relatives? It's too much of
you. You should stop it forthwith.

BIMPE: Right, husband, If you feel you can't meet my demands, You
should tell me gently Instead of disgracing me In your friends'
presence.

RAKINYO: That is not a disgrace at all. It's just a firm explanation to you
Of my new policy. No more demands for your people!

BIMPE: O.K., I am sorry I won't do so again. Gentlemen, here is water
To wash your hands in – And here is a towel for you.

ALHAJI AND NEKAN: Thank you so much. [*they finish eating*]

BIMPE: And fruits here please.

NEKAN: Oh, you have completed it! Thank you.

ALHAJI: Thank you, Bimpe. You have given us A royal treat.

BIMPE: Thank you for your appreciation.

RAKINYO: Thank you for your compliments. We hope to give you this opportunity From time to time.

ALHAJI: Rakinyo, the hour of worship Is fast approaching. We must go to the mosque. We will see you tomorrow If not after worship. Thank you.

NEKAN: Thank you, Rakinyo, Thank you, Bimpe.

RAKINYO: Thank you also. Let me get my driver To take you along. Bimpe, I shall return soon.

BIMPE: Right oh; good-bye.

ALL: Good-bye.

Rakinyo, Alhaji, and Nekan exit.

BIMPE: This is the first time Since I met him, That Rakinyo has complained That I ask too much For my relatives And for myself also. It is the first sign That shows me that Rakinyo's back-bone is breaking And the first signal That warns me that The tree-branch is weak – It is about to break; My bird must be prepared to fly. I have his fortune well in my hand. I am safe and secure. If he goes to court, Lawyer Kola is there for me. I must be sullen, disrespectful, harsh And unsympathetic. These will speed my expulsion From Rakinyo's house Before signs of poverty begin to show. I can thus save my face While I enjoy his vast wealth. Cunning, come to my side!

Rakinyo enters hurriedly through the door leading to the compound and calls in a horrified voice.

RAKINYO: Bimpe, Bimpe!

BIMPE: Yes, husband. Your voice has changed. Any horror?

RAKINYO: There is more than horror. My father's sickness has started again And it seems he has to see the doctor again.

BIMPE: Is that why you should be horrified? Send him to the hospital at once. Doctors are there to look after him.

RAKINYO: But . . . they won't attend to him.

BIMPE: Why will they not?

Rakinyo hesitates.

BIMPE: Take them to court if they refuse To perform the duty For which the government pays them.

RAKINYO: It's not that, Bimpe. The last hospital bill Has not been paid.
BIMPE: Why is that so? Pay the bill and give your father The chance to have the doctor's care.
RAKINYO: Bimpe, let me make a confession to you – A confession from the bottom of my heart. Rakinyo of yesterday Is not Rakinyo of today. The money that made Rakinyo Has gone to where it came from.
BIMPE: What are you saying, husband?
RAKINYO: If I pay the heavy hospital bill now, We shall have nothing to live upon.
BIMPE: And what are you going to do now, Rakinyo? What will the world think about you? How can you convince people That you were not dumping All that money into the sea?
RAKINYO: Bimpe, this should not alarm you. This is the time I expect my investments To come in handy.
BIMPE: If you invest somewhere, Why do you say you are poor?
RAKINYO: My investments are in you And in members of your family. Don't they say that good turns, Done to the right persons, Are investments Against black days? This is the time I expect you and your people To keep my name living.
BIMPE: Rakinyo, since the world began, Have you ever heard Of a woman feeding a man? You want to turn the world upside down By relying on a woman to feed you! For how long is this going to last?
RAKINYO: Is this your stand?
BIMPE: This is clear enough, Rakinyo. A man who had eaten The head of an elephant at meals, How can he be satisfied When a woman throws to him The head of a rat?
RAKINYO: Bimpe, you are saying all this – And to me?
BIMPE: But this is the plain truth. A woman can't be expected To maintain a man.
RAKINYO: If I had known in time That the tree I planted would refuse To support my weight In days of weakness, I wouldn't have planted it! If it had occurred to me earlier That the camel I trusted so well That I rejected other camels Would fail to carry me across the desert, I would not have bought it!
BIMPE: Rakinyo, don't speak like that. My camel is as trustworthy As any other. As for the truth, I will tell you plainly. Rakinyo, do something to save your face.

Rakinyo thinks awhile.

RAKINYO: Truly, something must be done To save my face. I shall commit suicide. If my father afterwards dies Uncared for, People would think It wouldn't have happened so If I had been alive. I bid you farewell, Bimpe. Let every property of mine Go to my family.

He starts to leave.

BIMPE: Come back Rakinyo. Is it not your father Who brought you into the world? How many of his age group Are living now? Let him die for you to live. Everybody prays For his child to bury him.

Rakinyo returns and thinks again.

RAKINYO: But how is this possible? The doctors – say the disease Cannot kill him easily.

Bimpe moves closer and lowers her voice.

BIMPE: This is a heart to heart talk. Go into the room and strangle him; Then come out and announce his death. You can then go on living while you take steps To improve your condition.

RAKINYO: What nonsense is that? I am not mad yet. I can't use my hand To kill my own father.

BIMPE: And so, I am the mad woman? I can now see clearly The trap you are setting for me. You made me speak my mind So that you might go round To broadcast it to your people And to the townsfolk as a whole That I want to kill your father. I must be gone from your house Before you spoil my stainless name.

RAKINYO: If you will go, you can go. I don't know what you take me for. You are advising me To go and strangle my father. Could you strangle yours'?

BIMPE: I see. You are bent On making me a scapegoat For your misfortune. I will quit before you have time To spoil my name.

RAKINYO: Nonsense! I can't listen To this silly talk any longer!

He leaves in annoyance.

BIMPE: Yiee! I am in a fix. I have committed myself. Whether I quit or not, So long as Rakinyo refuses To do as I bade him do, My name is not safe. If I don't want my name to be marred, It means I have to stay on with him, Using my money to keep him silent Over the issue. No, I can't imagine allowing Rakinyo To enjoy this money with me. Rakinyo must be made To meet my demand. But how? He is already decided not to do it. [*she reflects*] Yes, there is a way out. His aim is to rely on me for his livelihood. If I threaten to quit And I am firm on it, He will be forced to yield. This is the way! I must play it well.

Rakinyo enters.

RAKINYO: Are you still here?

BIMPE: I am only waiting To give you a last chance. Choose between doing as I bade you And my leaving you. Your decision is awaited.

RAKINYO: Will you stop this babbling And quit my house at once!

BIMPE: Right, I shall go into the room And give you some more time To think over the whole issue. But be sure that if I leave, You will regret it For the rest of your life. I am going to pack now.

She leaves. Rakinyo watches her go; he is confused.

RAKINYO: What a problem is this! This girl's threat is dangerous. If she quits now, I am finished. All my money will go with her And I shall be poorer than before! Yet how can I lay my hand On my own father?

Rakinyo sinks into a chair, dejected. Bimpe re-enters.

BIMPE: Well, Rakinyo, I am ready. Are you going to do it or not?

RAKINYO: I want to do it But it is difficult.

BIMPE: The answer I demand Is yes or no, Backed with action. Are you going to do it or not?

RAKINYO [*reflects and sighs*]: I will find it difficult, Bimpe.

BIMPE: You are not yet serious! Fare you well.

Rakinyo watches Bimpe as she goes out and cannot bear it any longer. He calls her back.

RAKINYO: Bimpe, come, don't go!

Bimpe returns.

BIMPE: Will you do it or not?

RAKINYO [*with difficulty*]: I . . . will . . . do . . . it.

BIMPE: Then be active. I will wait for you here.

Rakinyo walks hesitantly towards the door, stops and looks back at Bimpe with pleading eyes.

What is your hesitation for again? Do it and I stay. Refuse to do it And you lose me forever!

Rakinyo decides, and exits, but returns immediately.

RAKINYO: Bimpe, don't you think That people will know?

BIMPE: Don't be a child, husband. How will people know What you will do alone In the corner of your room?

RAKINYO: All right.

Exits but returns immediately again.

Bimpe, I overlooked one thing. If old man dies now, How do I get money for his funeral?

BIMPE: Never mind, I shall give it. Go in time.

Rakinyo exits.

BIMPE: May the devil fill his heart And blindfold him To do my wish! If he kills his father, And people get to know, My chance will be open To quit a murderer's house. If nobody knows it, I shall refuse to give The money for the funeral. A quarrel will follow And I shall be sacked Or get myself sacked. Luck, be my friend oh!
[*she moves to the door, peeps through, listens and returns*]
Will he do it . . . Or he will not . . .? I fear, if Rakinyo doesn't do it . . .

Rakinyo enters with bloodstains all over him.

Why? What about these bloodstains?

RAKINYO: You see, the old man was full of fight And wanted to shout. So I used a knife.

BIMPE: What? Why did you use a knife? I told you to strangle him and nothing else. But why did you do Something different? Did you do anything to control The spread of the blood?

RAKINYO: No. I was frightened. The whole room is bloodstained –
The blood of my own father! Ah!

BIMPE: This is foolish behaviour! See your jumper?

Rakinyo looks round his body.

RAKINYO: Oh, my jumper . . . My trousers . . . My leg . . . My hat too . . . I am dead!

BIMPE: Come along, husband; Don't be a child. There must be a way out . . . Does anybody know he is ill again?

RAKINYO: No.

BIMPE: Then go now and lock the corpse up And announce that he has travelled.

RAKINYO: To where?

BIMPE: To his mother's village Across River Powa.

RAKINYO: For the past ten years now, Old man has never travelled. And every relative knows He doesn't travel nowadays.

BIMPE: That is the more reason Why this scheme should work. People would say that on the only occasion He travelled in ten years He met his death. His death would thus Be attributed to fate; And you shall be safe.

RAKINYO: How can the corpse of a man, Dead in his mother's village,
Be under my roof With his throat cut? How do I explain this?
I am dead! I have behaved foolishly.

BIMPE: Don't be blind in the mind. In the dead of the night, You will
carry the corpse And throw it into Powa River. When the corpse is
discovered downstream, You don't have to explain anything.

RAKINYO: That is reasonable; I will do it. Then help me to cover the
corpse And clean the blood While I go to announce my father's
journey To his kinsmen in our family house.

BIMPE: No, I cannot.

RAKINYO: Oh Bimpe, aren't you going to assist me In any way?

BIMPE: Oh no, not that. But don't you know We women fear dead
bodies? I in particular fear blood More than a child.

RAKINYO: Well then, go and tell our relatives Of my father's journey.

BIMPE: No, this is not for me. This is an all-important issue Which
requires you, the old man's son. You understand your relatives better.
You know what tricks will work on them. If I go and I mar the case
now, You will be in danger. I don't want to have it said That your
wife led you into destruction. So I won't go. Do that yourself.

RAKINYO: All right. I will go to inform them And come back to pack
the corpse.

BIMPE: No, the corpse must be packed first, And you must be careful
In all your movements.

RAKINYO: Right, tell anybody who may call That I am out.

BIMPE: Leave that to me.

Rakinyo exits.

This is a scheme indeed – A scheme that has two sides. It can make
or unmake. But will it help me out of Rakinyo's house And thus
help me To enjoy my stock of wealth? Or will it ruin Rakinyo
And ruin me with him?

Bimpe exits.

SCENE FOUR

Four days later, Rakinyo and Bimpe are in Rakinyo's room.

RAKINYO: I am surprised, For four good days, Nobody has brought news
About old man's body!

BIMPE: If the body hangs where no man can see it, We may never hear of it again.

RAKINYO: If that happens, There will be plenty of sacrifices.

BIMPE: If there are sacrifices And the truth remains hidden, What do you care?

Kanbi enters rather noisily.

KANBI: Rakinyo, your ears, How many ?

RAKINYO: Two.

KANBI: I doubt it; for if they are two, You should have heard the news That has almost broken Every eardrum in the town now.

RAKINYO: What news, papa?

KANBI: Your father who travelled To Ilere four days ago Died in Powa River, And the body has been discovered at Ira, Ten miles down the river!

RAKINYO [*feigning surprise*]: What?

BIMPE: Oh, old man, What an end is this!

KANBI: The body was conveyed To the police station Where it was identified. From the police station, It was sent to the hospital Where it now is.

RAKINYO: Papa, is this how I am going to lose you – Unexpectedly – tragically – Without a single word of blessing? Oh, papa, papa, I did all I could To prevent this journey, But you were bent on going. Is it because your death called you Or is it because you wanted To be wicked to me?

KANBI: Stop there, Rakinyo; don't talk rubbish. This is clearly the work of fate. Some go by fire, others by water. He was to go by water, And seeing that his time was due, He went to where his way lay. If he had told you he was going to die, You wouldn't have let him go.

RAKINYO: True, papa, I wouldn't have let him go. For the past ten years, He never travelled that way. Why was he bent on going To Ilere this time? Truly, it is his death that called him. But how can I afford to miss him like that – A person I had lived with all my life!

KANBI: Come Rakinyo, you are grown now. Things should happen as they are now. It is he who should leave the back for you, For he brought you into the world. He has transferred the load of the aged to you. Find a suitable rag and carry it efficiently Till you also transfer it to your son.

RAKINYO: Thank you papa, I shall prove worthy of the load. Let us go to claim the corpse.

KANBI: I had sent for Ibitoye and Siju; I am sure they won't be long
to come. Let us wait for them.

A police sergeant is led in by Ode.

SERGEANT: Hello, Mr Rakinyo.

RAKINYO: Hello, Sergeant. Anything I can do for you?

SERGEANT: You are wanted at the police station.

RAKINYO: For what?

SERGEANT: I don't know. My duty is to take you there. I am sure you
will know everything When you reach the police station.

RAKINYO: And what about Ode? What is his duty with you?

SERGEANT: That is not your concern. You are to follow me to the
station, And that is all.

RAKINYO: Ode, since when did you join The Police Force?

ODE: I am still a hunter.

RAKINYO: And why are you here With the Sergeant?

ODE: Are you still asking me Such a question? Did I not meet you
Four days ago In the dead of the night Carrying a type of load
Towards the Powa River?

RAKINYO: And so you have stabbed me in the back! You of all people
have done this to me, Ode? Despite all your promises and vows
Which made me take you into confidence, You reported this case to
the police?

SERGEANT: Rakinyo, let's go. All statements should be made At the station.
[*he crosses over to take hold of Rakinyo*]

RAKINYO: Please Sergeant, hold on. I will go without force. Let me
have a word with my wife. Bimpe, this is the end of me. I am finished
Take good care of anything that is mine. My children and my
people Should not be ignored. Good-bye forever.

The Sergeant tries to lead Rakinyo out.

KANBI: Sergeant, please don't go yet. Rakinyo, what are you saying?
What is the matter Between you and Ode?

RAKINYO: Papa, rest your soul. Since Ode has come into the case, I am
finished. No amount of begging Can render any help.

KANBI: You are convinced You have gone against the law?

RAKINYO: I have gone against the law Of man and of God, And there
is no remedy now.

KANBI: What actually have you done? What is your off . . .

SERGEANT: Old man, get out of my way. I must take him to the
station Without delay.

KANBI: Sergeant wait, I beg you. [*Sergeant stops*] Please, could you see me Aside here for a minute?

SERGEANT: Oh, these people. You can worry people too much! [*goes over to Kanbi*]

KANBI: I know you are working For the Government, But your personal happiness Is more important.

SERGEANT: How?

KANBI: I mean . . . er . . . what I mean is . . . er . . . It . . . is . . er . . . well, Sergeant . . . er . . . Isn't it because of this same money That you are working?

SERGEANT: And what about it?

KANBI: No, Sergeant, I don't mean offence.

SERGEANT: What do you mean then?

KANBI: Oh . . . Sergeant. [*he laughs to please the Sergeant*] Don't be offended, This is nothing at all. After all, everybody does it these days.

SERGEANT: Everybody does what?

KANBI: Oh . . . Sergeant! Why do you want to torment me? I mean to be friendly, you see. [*he laughs nervously*]

SERGEANT: Torment you how? I am asking for your meaning.

KANBI: I see . . . er . . . I mean to say that The true happiness of a man today Rests with how much he is able to bag . . . I mean . . .

SERGEANT: I am happy with what I am given For my services. If I want more, I can work harder To earn promotion.

KANBI: Oh yes, I know that is easy For a popular person like you. But, you know, the true source of happiness Is that which comes in a big bulk. You see what I mean?

Ibitoye and Siju enter.

IBITOYE: Kanbi, why? What is happening?

KANBI: They say Rakinyo has gone Against the law And he has been arrested by the Sergeant.

SIJU: Gone against the law how? Is it an offence against the law To stay in one's room? This boy has not gone outside his room For weeks past. Don't you Government people Want him to live again? Here, his father has just met his end And instead of sympathizing with him You are doubling his sorrows By weaving lies around his legs. You policemen are callous!

SERGEANT: Ei, woman, mind what you say! If you don't take care, I will arrest you also now For obstructing me in my duty.

SIJU: All right, take him away And do whatever you like with him.

Maybe it is a crime for him to exist at all. You who can destroy life
But cannot restore it!

SERGEANT: Come on, move on!

He pushes Rakinyo out. Siju is weeping.

SIJU: An innocent child Being treated like a murderer! He lives among
his kinsmen, And yet, he is treated like a stranger – Like an orphan!
Have you ever seen such a treatment? People have grown rich in
this town And in the surrounding towns before . . . None of them
has fallen victim To this type of jealousy. Why is it that it is only
our son Who is singled out By the common men And by the
Government people? [*she weeps*]

IBITOYE: As for you women And your childish way of life! How do you
think weeping Can save Rakinyo now? Please return home And let
us have time to think. You did not exercise patience. You annoyed
the policeman And now he has taken him away. You didn't give us
time to find out Our son's offence. You gave us no breathing space
To know how to see the policeman. Now you start to weep, Confusing
the matter more and more. Please, leave us alone!

SIJU: Are you telling me Not to bring out What is in my mind? I will do
so. I will tell them That what they are doing Is not good!

IBITOYE: And what have you brought Out of that? Confusion!

SIJU: I have spoken my mind And that is all!

Alhaji and Nekan enter.

IBITOYE: Ah, Alhaji, Nekan, you are welcome. Your friend has been
arrested by the police For an offence. She [*indicating Siju*] didn't give
us a chance To find out. Come and think with us. What are we to do?

NEKAN: Which of them arrested him?

SIJU: It's Sergeant, oh . . . Sergeant! That bad man. We spoke, he said
he would arrest us too. A wicked man; A jealous man. I don't know
what he is out for. Howu! Should Rakinyo not exist?

ALHAJI: All right mama, keep cool. Was there any other officer In his
company?

KANBI: No, only Ode who led him here Was with him.

ALHAJI: Do you say he has been taken To the police station?

KANBI: I am sure, to the police station.

ALHAJI: All right, we will go to see Inspector. You must get some money
ready. You know the police, The bigger the case is, The bigger must
be the fist You will clench.

IBITOYE: As for the fist, We shall make it as big As the case may
    demand. Our son has not been lazy.

ALHAJI: Nekan, let's go.

Alhaji and Nekan exit.

IBITOYE: Well wife, what do you know About your husband's case?

BIMPE: Papa, why ask me this sort of question? You are in the world,
    I am also in the world, And you are asking me About heaven.
    How can I know this?

SIJU: Kai re!* Have you no eye lashes? Don't you know That this is
    your husband's father? Why that cheeky answer?

BIMPE: Mama, how else do you want me To answer that sort of
    question?

SIJU: If you . . .

KANBI: Please Siju, keep cool. This is not the time for quarrels. Let us
    push everything aside Till after the case When we shall demand
    An explanation for everything.

IBITOYE: The police arrested him, In your presence, wife. What charges
    were brought against him?

BIMPE: Well, he was accused of carrying a load, In the dead of the night
    four days ago, Towards the River Powa. Sergeant Ode, who led the
    Sergeant here, Met him carrying the load.

IBITOYE: What type of load was it?

BIMPE: This is the type of question I say I can't possibly answer!

IBITOYE: All right wife, listen to me here. Did Rakinyo not say a word
    of protest Or throw any light on the whole affair?

BIMPE: Well, your son seemed to have been guilty; For he accepted
    responsibility for everything Without hesitating for a moment.
    Especially since Ode came onto the scene. He bade me farewell.
    Thereupon, papa took the matter up.

KANBI: Although you said we should not Ask you questions again,
    I will ask this. Did Rakinyo sleep in the house Four nights ago or not?

BIMPE: I am sure I bade him goodnight Before I went to bed, And
    greeted him good morning The following morning when I woke up.
    If this amounts to sleeping in the house, Then he slept here that
    night.

IBITOYE: And did he get out in the night After you went to bed?

BIMPE: How on earth, could I know this When I was not a watchman?

*Kai re – A rebuke, especially a much younger wrong-doer who contra-
dicts a serious tradition.

SIJU: You should know. You should know I say! You are his wife And
you stay here with him.

BIMPE: And what about that? He has his room and I have mine. I had
no cause to keep watch on him. Why then should I keep awake
To know if he would sneak out or not?

KANBI: This one also should not be allowed To lead to quarrels in any
form. Wife, the urgent need now is that Money should be provided
for the police As Alhaji said before he left. So, try to go in. We are
waiting for you here.

BIMPE: I am sorry, I don't know where he keeps his money.

KANBI: Don't you have anything on you? I mean . . . something like
chop money And other petty amounts you can gather For this
emergency case?

BIMPE: Do you mean his money or mine?

KANBI: It doesn't matter where it comes from. If a man sees a snake
And a woman kills it, It matters not So long as the snake does not
escape.

BIMPE: I cannot touch my money On account of this case.

SIJU: What do you say? Say it again And let me hear!

BIMPE: I say my farthing Shan't go into this case.

SIJU: Even if he is going to be jailed?

BIMPE: Even if he is going to be hanged.

They exchange looks of surprise.

KANBI: So you are not concerned at all?

BIMPE: Why should I be concerned? He brought it upon himself. If he
hadn't carried a load In the dead of the night, Who would dare to
arrest Rakinyo?

SIJU: You can kill your husband, you! You ate good things with him . . .
Enjoyed life with him And when trouble comes, You want to
dissociate yourself From him! You are a witch!

BIMPE: Come mama, let me tell you, This is the disease of all of us. If
Rakinyo had invited you To come and swim in his money, You
would have come. Wouldn't you? If Rakinyo was to be buried,
Would you have agreed To be buried with him? Therefore, weigh
yourself properly Before judging others.

KANBI: You, you, you are not a good wife!

BIMPE: I agree. And he is also not a good husband.

KANBI: You have no regard for anybody, And I am going to make sure
that Rakinyo divorces you after the case.

BIMPE: Divorce me on his behalf now And you will see me gone By the
  next wink of the eye!

KANBI: That is all. I am going to carry out Your wish.

He sees Alhaji and Nekan entering.

  You are welcome. How much do we need?

ALHAJI: You don't need anything but a coffin.

IBITOYE: Have they released old man's corpse?

NEKAN: Hold on, Alhaji. Let the women go out Before you continue.

KANBI: Siju, you go home. We shall tell you What the outcome is.

SIJU: I shall go.

Siju leaves.

NEKAN: What about Bimpe?

KANBI: Go on without minding that one. I don't regard her as a human
  being.

BIMPE: Right, you regard me as wood And I am going to show you
  The behaviour of wood today.

KANBI: You can't surprise me by that For I have told you already,
  I don't regard you as a human being.

BIMPE: Neither do I regard you as one!

ALHAJI: Ah, Bimpe! Is there any stage of lunacy That makes fire
  undiscernible? Don't you know this old man To be your husband's
  father?

KANBI: Alhaji, don't mind her. She is no more Rakinyo's wife. Go
  on.

ALHAJI: Bimpe, you have made me dumb You have made my senses
  dead. I don't even know how to go on.

NEKAN: Papa, not to waste time, You have rightly said That Bimpe
  shall no longer Be Rakinyo's wife.

KANBI: That is it! If you, Rakinyo's friends, Also see that I am not
  being childish Because of old age, I am happy. Let us go back to
  the original point We were discussing. You said we shall need a
  coffin For the old man's corpse?

ALHAJI: Papa, you will need two.

IBITOYE: Two coffins for only one body? Don't make a joke of this
  matter.

ALHAJI: It is no joke papa. You will need one for the old man And the
  other for his son, Rakinyo!

IBITOYE AND KANBI: What?

KANBI: Please speak to me With the true tongue Of an Omo Oduduwa.* For whom do you say The other coffin is?

ALHAJI: For Rakinyo, papa. Rakinyo is dead! [*he bows his head*]

KANBI: Rakinyo is dead also! What else am I left with? Death, You that snatch the beloved princes, And visit a mother of ten, Leaving her with no child! You that enter a populous house And leave it empty! When will you stop this fight In our family! [*he wipes his eyes*]

IBITOYE: Rakinyo is dead!

NEKAN: Papa, take heart And be a man Ask for the cause Of Rakinyo's sudden death And how it came about.

KANBI: Thank you, my son. I am a man And so shall I remain. What caused his death?

NEKAN: Rakinyo had committed the greatest crime The world has ever heard of; And he confessed it before swallowing The poison which killed him. It was Rakinyo who killed his father! To cover up, he announced That his father had travelled. That very night, he threw the body Into the sacred River Powa. Unfortunately for Rakinyo. He was caught by Ode Who was coming from his hunting rounds. Ode reported the case to the police And Rakinyo was arrested. This is the sad story we have for you.

KANBI: This is a great crime indeed!

IBITOYE: A crime such as the ear Has never heard of before!

There is dead silence for some time. Kanbi takes a deep breath and speaks.

KANBI: All right, whatever step we shall take, One thing must be done first. This devil of a woman must be sacked And Rakinyo's property protected.

BIMPE: I have told you I am ready To sever relationships with Rakinyo And his family at any time.

ALHAJI: Papa, please be patient in this matter. Is it not the custom in our land That when a man dies, his wife is given To his younger next of kin. Let us start from there So that we bear no blame.

KANBI: Thank you my son. You have spoken well. I lost the control of my emotion Because she proved too much For my nerves. Ibitoye, what is your view?

IBITOYE: There is much sense in the suggestion. So go ahead.

KANBI: Wife, your husband is dead, Yet he is living. He is living in the persons Of his younger brothers Who have reached manhood. Make your choice among them And that will be our choice for you.

---

*Omo Oduduwa, the son of Oduduwa – the father of the Yorubas.

BIMPE: I am not prepared to marry Any other person in the family.

ALHAJI: You don't mean it!

BIMPE: I mean it!

ALHAJI: You don't mean it. You will not go away And tell people you were ousted After your husband's death Without being given a fair chance.

BIMPE: Who will do that – myself? It is by my own free will That I am quitting the family.

ALHAJI: Then it is a devilish free will!

BIMPE: Look this man, Why is your deep interest in the case? Even if you are a member of the family, Yours' shouldn't be so hard. And, gentleman, if you have a secret hope Of monetary gain Out of my second marriage Into the family, Declare it now!

ALHAJI: A hope of monetary gain . . . me?

BIMPE: If you don't have the hope, Then wash your hands of The affair of a family To which you don't belong.

ALHAJI: Right, thank you. Papa, that is your wife. Whatever you like You can do with her, My friend and I will go To see to the corpses Which indeed we are connected with. Nekan, let's go.

Alhaji and Nekan exit, greatly annoyed.

IBITOYE: Er . . . wife, there should be No more waste of time. Declare to us now, With sufficient proof, Which articles are yours And which are Rakinyo's. You shall be free thereafter To go with your belongings.

BIMPE: Excuse me, old men. Which things do you classify As Rakinyo's?

IBITOYE: What silly question is that? Can the eye not gauge What quantity of food Will satisfy the stomach?

BIMPE: All right, gauge on. I will tell you Where you go wrong.

Kola, Bimpe's lawyer, enters.

Oh, welcome, Lawyer. There my lawyer comes. He is the person You have to deal with now.

KOLA: Good evening, old men; Good evening, Bimpe. Accept my sympathy On the death of your husband. I heard, a short while ago, And I thought of calling on you. But why your reference to me?

BIMPE: There they are, Rakinyo's uncles. They say I should bring my head Because I refuse to marry Into their family a second time.

KOLA: Oh, how?

IBITOYE: Lawyer, never mind her. We only told her to hand over Rakinyo's belongings to us If she leaves our family.

BIMPE: And I told you to tell me what things You consider belong to
Rakinyo. For, as far as I am concerned, Rakinyo had nothing more
To lay claim upon.

IBITOYE: What do you mean? What about those seven-ton lorries, That
carry palm oil to the north And bring cattle to us here?

BIMPE: He sold them long before his death. However, the drivers were
still retained By their new owners.

IBITOYE: To whom did he sell them?

BIMPE: I don't know all, But I bought two of them.

KANBI: You bought two of the lorries? I can't believe it.

BIMPE: Lawyer, if you have the papers here, Kindly show them their
son's fingerprint Concerning the sale.

The lawyer searches through his file and brings out some papers.

KOLA: Old men, I have the papers here. Your son actually sold Two of
his lorries to her But they agreed to keep it secret.

KANBI: Lawyer!

KOLA: It is true. Here are the papers; Book never lies

*The lawyer hands over the papers. Ibitoye and Kanbi look through them, but are
unable to understand them.*

KANBI: Machine has been used to write this; The language used is
strange to us; But the hand of our son Is well known to us. Lawyer,
why is it that He did not write his name under it In his own hand?

KOLA: In important legal issues like this, Thumb print is more relied
upon, For it cannot be denied. Rakinyo, for example, could sign this
paper, Using a different handwriting. He could deny the ownership
Of the signature at a later date. So, the thumb print you see there
Is sufficient proof.

KANBI: Hmm . . . but now that he is dead, What can we do . . . What
can we say?

KOLA: I am sorry papa, I cannot advise you What to do or what to say.

KANBI: Oh, Lawyer, I didn't mean To seek your advice. I was only
thinking aloud.

KOLA: I see.

IBITOYE: Well, Bimpe, if you have bought His big lorries, What about
his pleasure car? We shall take that from you!

BIMPE: He ceased to be the owner of the car Only last week.

IBITOYE: Have you bought that one also?

BIMPE: No. It was bought by my brother.

KANBI: Your brother?

BIMPE: My brother.

KANBI: On credit?

BIMPE: He paid the money on the spot.

IBITOYE: Then why is the car Still in Rakinyo's garage?

BIMPE: Do you call that Rakinyo's garage?

IBITOYE: It's clearly his.

BIMPE: You will soon understand That part also. But the reason The car still remains here Is that my brother went on a trek Soon after buying it And he is not expected back Till next week.

KANBI: Your brother bought the car Cash down?

BIMPE: Cash down.

KANBI: Are there papers about this also?

BIMPE: Lawyer, please show them the papers.

KOLA: Here they are, old men.

Ibitoye and Kanbi glance through them again in bewilderment and without understanding them.

KANBI: How is it, Bimpe, That all members of your family Grew so wealthy, Soon after you married Rakinyo, That they could buy the whole world Cash down?

BIMPE: You can't ask me that question. Is my brother not working? Or do you hear that he breeds Money-eating fowls?

IBITOYE: Truly your brother works, And he does not swallow money. But we have seen people Who held higher posts Before your brother finished school And yet cannot even buy the type of a lorry, Cash down or not. We also know your brother's post In their office today!

BIMPE: If people grow rich with age, You old men could have been Twenty times richer than Rakinyo! Or does the length of service Dictate a man's ability to save money?

KANBI: All right, we shall waste no more time. Hand us the papers on his cattle In the north.

BIMPE: As far as I know, He has no head of cattle In the north.

IBITOYE: Who then is the owner of the herd His name is attached to?

BIMPE: Lawyer, kindly show them the papers. They all bear my name.

IBITOYE: He put your name on the papers Only to beat down the tax. That doesn't give you the right To claim the cattle herd.

BIMPE: If that is what he told you, He has told you a lie. I spent my own money And my own energy To secure the herd. A single finger-print of his Is not on the papers.

KANBI: And so you are grabbing this also?

KOLA: Please, old man, Let us pick the words we use Very carefully. And mind how we use them. Your use of the word 'grab' Is very damaging. You cannot prove your claim Whereas she has documentary proof Of legal ownership of the herd. If this matter goes to court now, She can claim a heavy sum from you On charges of defamation of character. You see my point of argument?

KANBI: Thank you Lawyer. I withdraw the word 'grab'. But kindly tell her To pack her belongings And quit this house now.

BIMPE: The house in which we are now Or another?

KANBI: This one in which we are.

BIMPE: Why?

IBITOYE: If Rakinyo has lost Every other fruit of his labour To you by law, Should we leave the only one That is unquestionably his To you again?

BIMPE: This house is also not Rakinyo's.

IBITOYE: As for this, you shan't have it. If there are also papers Which will make you claim this house, We shall set law aside. Better die like a rat Than live a subject of public ridicule! This one – for your brother! That one – for your mother! Every other thing – for yourself! Why? Does it mean that Rakinyo had never existed? Law, law, law; everything is law. Say this – they say it is law! Say that – they say it is law! Are we white men?

KOLA: Old man, don't be so annoyed. She can explain the situation.

IBITOYE: She can go on explaining. I know she has law papers For this also.

KOLA: Don't let this worry you. It is the present days' demand. Bimpe, explain it to them.

BIMPE: Some creditors came two months ago And would take a court action Unless Rakinyo paid them. To prevent disgrace, Rakinyo approached me With a proposal to sell this house In order to raise funds To clear the debt. I bought the house there and then, And here is Lawyer Kola, our witness.

KOLA: The papers are here. [*he brings out more papers*]

IBITOYE: We are no more interested In your papers. He who does not believe in God, There is no need persuading him With Jesus.

KANBI: Hmm . . . hmm . . . the white men have truly tried! They have done much for the black world By teaching us to read and write; They have taught us to be wise – Too wise for our race. Everything is by law – the white man's law! It is possible for the fruit of one man's labour To belong to another man Who can tender papers in evidence! Is this slavery? Is it cheating? Gods of the black race, Are you asleep?

IBITOYE: Rise and let us go, brother. They have the white man's law

Firmly on their side, Forgetting that the black man, Before the
advent of the white man, Had laws of his own, Governing his own
society. Young woman, I shall teach you To know and respect the
black man's laws. Then we shall see who is being deceived, You or
ourselves.

Kola and Bimpe watch Ibitoye and Kanbi leave.

KOLA: Well, the task is well accomplished.
BIMPE: Exactly as I want it done! But Lawyer, I fear that man's
speech. His last words were treacherous.
KOLA: Why should you fear, Bimpe, Where there is no fear? Who is
the author Of the book of African law From which he will teach
you? Forget about him and let's think About the booty we have.
BIMPE: I can't forget about him, Lawyer. Your skin only is black, You
are white in your mind. I cannot fail to remember The black man's
power.
KOLA: Will he beat you, Or will he kill you? The law is there to check
him And that's all for that.
BIMPE: I'm afraid, I fear still. Truly, if he beats me Or attempts to kill
me The law will punish him. But can the African not kill In a way
the law can't prove? This is what I fear, Lawyer.
KOLA: Look, woman, I haven't time For all this nonsense. My
involvement in this case, As is well known to you, Is to help you
and no more. And see what a coward you are!
BIMPE: I am sorry Lawyer, To inconvenience you. Let us go ahead To
share everything As we pre-arranged.
KOLA: Definitely not now, Bimpe. We arranged, Not being able to guess
To what extent our success would be. Documents have to be
prepared And duly signed by you and me, Before the sharing can
be done.

Bimpe holds her chest in pain.

BIMPE: Lawyer . . . but . . . help . . . chest . . . my chest!
KOLA: Chest how? What is happening?

*Kola feels her chest as Bimpe breathes hard and sprawls on the ground, unable to
talk. He runs across the room, looking for help.*

KOLA: Who is there! Who is there!

*Eventually, he returns to sit down, holding the head of the hard-breathing Bimpe
on his lap. She takes a deep breath and is silent.*

KOLA: Is this how you end it, Bimpe? I am sorry for you though, Yet if
it is not bad for one person, It cannot be good for another. The
need to cheat you in my final draft Is no more. Death has cheated
you More than I can ever do. What should have belonged to two
Will now belong to one. Bimpe, sleep well!

*He puts Bimpe's head down gently and rises. Dewale calls from outside as he
enters into the room.*

DEWALE: Kola!

KOLA: Yes, Dewale. [*rushing to meet Dewale at the door*]

DEWALE: Your driver is dead In a motor accident!

KOLA: How, Dewale?

DEWALE: He knocked your car Against a heavy truck, And the car is
shattered into pieces!

KOLA: Ha!

DEWALE: It is a big loss I know, But you have to take heart.

KOLA: I shall take heart, For there is a compensation for me
Greater than ten times the car.

DEWALE: How? What do you mean?

KOLA: We have succeeded in grasping all Er . . . er . . . as you know . . .
As I told you!

DEWALE: How on earth, Kola? Did you get all?

KOLA: We got everything! And there, I struck luck within luck.

DEWALE: Luck within luck?

KOLA: Luck within luck, Dewale. Soon after Rakinyo's frustrated uncles
left, Swearing, cursing and threatening, Bimpe developed a chest
complaint Which sent her to silence; Thus leaving everything to
me – Me alone!

DEWALE: Bimpe dead!

KOLA: There lies her corpse [*they move near it*]

DEWALE: And you maintain that She died soon after the old men left?

KOLA: Not very long after.

DEWALE: And the old men left dissatisfied?

KOLA: Yes.

DEWALE: Threatening and swearing?

KOLA: Empty threats anyway. And they vowed to teach Bimpe To know
the black man's law.

DEWALE: Kola, is it possible that your long stay In the white man's
country Has made you blind Has made it impossible for you To see
life with the African eye? Can't you perceive that the gathering
cloud Is a sign of an approaching rain? Would you fail to understand

That the death which kills one's age-group And snatches one's contemporary Is giving a proverbial warning That one's time is also at hand? A witch cried yesterday And a child died today; Who does not know That it was yesterday's witch Who killed the child? Here is big money for you indeed.

KOLA: Yes, very, very big money! [*brightens up*]

DEWALE: But by this money Lies your life!

KOLA: My life? [*he is frightened and confused*]

DEWALE: Yes, your life! Choose one And lose the other.

KOLA: What is your meaning? [*more frightened*]

DEWALE: I'll talk no more. Half a word Is all that is necessary For a child who will do well. Inside him, the half word turns whole. Thank you. Make your choice.

Dewale exits.

KOLA: Dewale, don't go! Wait, advise me! But . . . [*he turns round in confusion, takes two strides in an attempt to run away, but checks himself and falls into deep thought*] There is big money on one side – Yes, big money. I can see that! [*gleeful*] But my life on the other – [*frightened*] My life – no! [*picks up some of the papers hurriedly which had blown out of his hand, and attempts to run away but checks himself*] But this money is really big! [*he brightens up again and returns slowly*] Ah, my life is by its side! [*in fear, he sinks into a chair, sweating profusely and breathing heavily*] Ei, what is that? [*holding his chest*] Is that the chest complaint? No, not me. Yieeeee! The chest pain! My chest! My chest! No, no, no, I don't want the house any more. I don't want anything any more! Oh, my head, my head! [*holding his head*] I will choose my life now I don't want big money any more! Stomach . . . my stomach . . .! My rib . . .! rib . . .! rib . . .! Dewale come, come . . . save me . . .! Yeeee! My back . . . waist . . . back-bone! I am fainting! Dewale come and save me . . . Please . . . Dewale help, help . . .! [*he collapses, sprawls, and breathes hard; then he dies*]

Dewale enters and calls from the entrance.

DEWALE: Kola! Kola! [*he sees Kola's body*] Kola why? You also dead! I can't believe it. [*he rushes to the spot, lifts Kola's head, and sees that he is dead*] How is a man better Than a spike of grass If his life can be lost As easily as a child's plaything? Wherein lies man's importance Among other creatures If his life cannot resist death Any more than an ant's . . .? What is the significance of a human If he could chat, laugh, be ambitious, And, in the wink of an eye, pass away, Laying his life at the foot of his ambition . . .? Big money . . . Big car . . . Big house . . . To which of you Do these belong now? To none! Kola, what a parting is this After many years' friendship? You have died a death that was avoidable – A death you brought upon yourself, I shall miss you in my life Sleep well . . . And you, the devil incarnate, The messenger of death; May your soul rest in peace, Or in pieces.

He returns to Kola's body, kneels by it and inspects the face. He goes over to Bimpe's body; then comes back to Kola's body.

Oh, Kola, is this how you like it . . .?

He sings in form of dirge as people come on to carry the bodies off.

Oduduwa, father of all
*That greet 'E̱ ku aro̱; e̱ jire',**
Show us your mercy
That those of us left behind
May successfully hold the fort.
This house has turned out
To be a house of blood
As if blood built it.
Now, blood must purify it.
Yes; blood, not of hen,
But of white sheep –
White and healthy sheep
Seven pigeons
Must be sacrificed
To the originators
Of Rakinyo's family.
This must be done,
And done immediately
If blood is not to draw on
More blood.

---

*E̱ ku aro̱; e̱ jire – Yoruba morning greeting which translates: 'Good morning; hope you wake up well' (i.e. in good health).